ONLY IN HONG KONG

NURY VITTACHI

An Incom?rehens!ble Book

An INCOM?REHENS!BLE Book

ONLY IN HONG KONG
© Nury Vittachi 1993

ISBN 962-10-0152-8

Cover design by Jed Donohoe

Typeset by South China Morning Post Publishers Ltd

Printed by Printflex Hong Kong

Fifth Impression, December 1994

All rights reserved. This book is sold subject to the condition that it shall not, by way of trade or otherwise, be lent, resold, hired out, or otherwise circulated without the publisher's prior consent in any form of binding or cover other than that in which it is published and without a similar condition including this condition being imposed on the subsequent purchaser.

CONTENTS

You Are Entering – The Twilight Zone, **1**
Only in Hong Kong, **9**
The Average Asian's Attention Span is So Short These Days that He Frequently Starts a Sentence But Forgets to, **28**
A Serious Warning About a Grave Danger We Are All In, **31**
We Hand Out Some Awards, **35**
Why Men Don't Have Abdomens, **43**
Misdirected Male, **47**
Hitler Wong and the Hung Fat Brassiere Company, **50**
Lord of All He Surveys, **74**
What Every Traveller in Asia Should Know, **78**
Smart Machines and Smart-Alec Machines, **103**
True Stories, **106**
And Moses Told Them to Take Some Tablets . . . , **121**
Why Compromise? Get Divorced Instead, **123**
Peking Order, **126**
Asians Make Important Technological Advances, Like Wearable Vitamins, **142**
Dr Doom's Abbreviated Tail of Woe, **145**
Misprunts, **149**
Home Sweet Hotel, **160**

Alarming Devices, **164**

Broker and Broker Still, **167**

Run! The Lawyers Are Revolting, **184**

Human Writes, **188**

The Cat Who Learned the Fax of Life, **192**

SEX, or, You Flipped to This Section First, Didn't You?, **194**

Commercial Break, **198**

At Last: A Cure for Love, **208**

Foreign Exchange, **217**

The New Age Dawns in Asia, **222**

Smart Cocktails, Stupid Drinkers, **225**

Headhunting For Real Heads, **228**

Made in Asia: Tomorrow's Products − Tomorrow, **230**

Car-oke For Beginners, **242**

Adventures in the Property Trade, **248**

Beautiful Homes and Gardens With Funny Shaped Hedges, **253**

Toys for Modern Children and Other Dangerous Lunatics, **257**

Twisted Humour, **263**

Naming of Parts, **267**

PREFACE

I have only one cast-iron, rock-solid, unassailable, hard and fast rule in my life, and it is this:

I have no cast-iron, rock-solid, unassailable, hard and fast rules in my life.

The fact that I actually have one proves that I don't, if you see what I mean.

My other hard and fast rule is to try and tell the truth whenever I can. In your hands is a book of bizarre stories – but they are all real-life tales gathered from Hong Kong and its neighbours. Many of the anecdotes appear light-hearted and trivial, but taken as a whole, they become a record of two major movements:

1. The gathering here of people from mismatched cultures to make plastic watches and be hailed in the West as builders of an Economic Miracle.

2. Asia-Pacific's headlong rush from the age of the rickshaw (average speed: 3 mph) to the age of the futuristic turbo-charged traffic jam (average speed: 2½ mph).

Some people have described me, in an accusatory tone, as a "tabloid journalist". Although I hope I have more scruples than the less principled of my brethren in that line of work, I admit to having many of the traits of the tabloid newshound.

I opt for human interest stories. I write in short sentences.

I do little tricks to hold the reader's attention. One of my favourite is to add an enormous amount of acid emphasis to a paragraph by repeating a sentence in italics. I'm sure you know exactly what I mean. *I'm sure you know exactly what I mean.*

I have tried to avoid being too much of a linguistic chauvinist, although I have been unable to completely disregard the intrinsic humour in the thousands of tiny misunderstandings and adjustments which have to be made when cultures learn to live together.

A friend of mine stepped into a restaurant in Bangkok recently, and ordered what he found written at the top of the menu: "Joke of the Day". Many Asians will immediately guess what was intended: juk, which is Chinese congee, or rice-soup.

But he ordered it, and so received some nourishment as well as a laugh. If I provide a service a fraction as good as that street cafe, I will be well satisfied.

My style of journalism, more than most, relies on contributions from readers. So thank you for the thousands of letters, and don't stop sending them to publications wherever you see my name.

I am also happy to receive criticism or complaints. But this is also not a hard and fast rule.

NURY VITTACHI
Hong Kong
September 1993

To Mary

**YOU ARE ENTERING – THE TWILIGHT ZONE
(DOO DEE DOO DOO, DOO DEE DOO DOO)**

He meant well: Phoned a Hong Kong oil company executive on a weekday late afternoon.
    Lai See: Is Mr Wong there, please?
    Staff member: Get out.
    Lai See: !
    Staff member: Get out.
    Lai See: Do you mean 'Gone home?'
    Staff member: Yes.
    Receptionist training has a long way to go in Hong Kong.

Operatic masterpiece: Brian Parker of Kim Eng Securities phoned the Arts Festival Hotline in Hong Kong.
    Brian: Hello. Can I book two tickets for *Tosca* please?
    Hotline: Sorry. Oscar he on holiday.
    (Click.)

Time traveller: Alan Skyrme of Hong Kong Bank was on the phone trying to get hold of a contact in a Tsim Sha Tsui export firm.

Secretary: Mr Chan's office.

Skyrme: Is he available?

Secretary: He is out of town. He is due back from his trip yesterday.

Skyrme: If he is due back yesterday, can I get hold of him?

Secretary: Please call back yesterday.

And be on time: Paul Frankland, manager of the Hong Kong office of Commercial Union Assurance, rang Maurice Gardette's French restaurant, Cafe De Paris in Lan Kwai Fong.

Frankland: My name is Frankland. I wish to cancel my reservation for tonight.

Staff member (looking in the book): You have a reservation for two people at 8 pm.

Frankland: Yes. I wish to cancel it.

Staff member: May I have your telephone number?

Frankland: Why do you need my telephone number if I am cancelling my reservation? Anyway, it's 525 5245 if you're interested.

Staff member: Okay. Thanks. See you tonight!

Little Beasts: Ram Sajnani of Reena Enterprises went to Pizza Hut in Tsim Sha Tsui to arrange a birthday party for his son. He asked a manageress how much it would cost per person for his family and his son's friends.

"Same price, HK$33, for both children and humans," she replied.

They cater for all sorts at Pizza Hut.

Warm reception: Enzo Pesci of the Retkie Group was in

Italy, making a long distance call to his Hong Kong office.
 Pesci: Good morning. I am Mr Pesci. Can I speak with . . .
 Receptionist: I am sorry. Mr Pesci is in Italy. But if you leave your name and telephone number . . .
 Pesci: I KNOW Mr Pesci is in Italy because I AM Mr Pesci.
 Receptionist: Well, in that case, you do not need to leave your name and your number.

Plain Jane: Philippa Robeson of Aberdare Consultants phoned the new KPS Video Express store in Admiralty.
 KPS: You would like to reserve a movie?
 Philippa: Yes please. *Jean de Florette.* (spells) J.E.A.N., D.E.,
 KPS: *Jonathan!*
 Philippa: No. Please wait and listen. *Jean de Florette.* J.E.A.N. New word. D.E.
 KPS: *Jane de Fonda!*

Most baffled receptionist: Colin Robertson of the Commission for Canada in Hong Kong decided to call his office.
 Robertson: This is Colin Robertson. I'd like to speak to —
 Receptionist: Mr Robertson is not here.
 Robertson: No. THIS is Mr Robertson. I want —
 Receptionist: Why are you calling yourself?

Least ruffle-able shopgirl: Patrick Tuohy of Clerical Medical International was in the Prince's Building branch of KPS Video Express when he saw a customer reach the desk.
 Customer: I've left my membership card in the office.
 KPS: Can you remember your name?
 Customer: !
 (After a pause)

Customer (sarcastic): Sorry, but it's on my card in the office.

KPS (unruffled): Okay. What about your phone number?

Shock reply: All the electricity went off in the Cheng Sha area of Lantau during recent storms, we heard from resident Craig Sanderson.

His neighbour phoned Park'N Shop supermarket to see if it was open. He asked if they had any electricity.

"No sir," replied the staff member. "We don't sell electricity."

Secret service: A colleague of ours phoned Hawley and Hazel Chemical Co in Wong Chuk Hang.

Very pleasant receptionist (VPR): Good morning! Hawley and Hazel!

Caller: Good morning. Do you have a public relations department?

VPR: No, we don't.

Caller: Do you use an agency for your public relations?

VPR: Yes, we do.

Caller: Can I have their name and their telephone number?

VPR: No. I am sorry. That information is confidential.

If Hawley and Hazel's PR firm is reading this, now you know why you never get any referrals.

Dry Martini: Hong Kong socialite Ms Chantal Slim was on the phone trying to contact Antonio Maria Martini from Lux Collezioni.

Mrs Slim: Can I speak to Mr Martini?

Reception: He is out for lunch.

Mrs Slim: Can you ask him to return the call of Mrs Slim?

Reception: I am sorry. Mrs Slim is out to lunch.

Most thorough shop assistant: Toymaker Bob Dorsee of Tyco Hong Kong bought some crew-neck shirts at Ocean Terminal, paying by credit card. The shop clerk asked him to sign a handwritten receipt and the printed cash register slip.

Then she carefully compared the signature on the receipt with the one on the credit card. They matched. Then she carefully compared the signature on the cash register slip with the one on the credit card.

"It was just in case I had transmogrified on the spot between signings," said Bob.

Chamber maid: Hugh Chambers of Hong Kong Telecom CSL had some family in town, also surnamed Chambers. His wife Karen returned to the hotel room where they live, in the Grand Plaza in Kornhill, to see the message light blinking.

She phoned down to the reception.

Karen: You have a message for me?

Reception: No. Only the message you left for yourself.

Karen: I haven't left a message for myself. What message is that?

Reception: "Call Mrs Chambers".

Load of CAC: A computer firm called CAC-System is sending out junk faxes to offices in Hong Kong advertising their products. We liked quite a lot of the stuff, but there was no address to write to. We phoned them.

Lai See: Good morning. Can we have your address please?

CAC: What?

Lai See: I would like your address please, to send you a letter.

CAC: Do you want some information about our products?

Lai See: I'd like your address.

CAC: Ah. Er. Leave your number and someone will call you back.

Lai See: Don't you know your address?

CAC: Someone will call you back on that.

How do CAC staff get to work if they don't know their address? Do they all live on the premises?

Bamboozled: Went to a party at the Regent on May 4, 1992, to watch a giant sculpture called The Bamboo Man sail down the harbour in an "art event".

Larry Zuckerman of the *International Herald Tribune* was as opened-mouthed at the sight as we were. "And we thought the eighties were over . . ." he said.

Meanwhile on the other side of the harbour, Helen Baily of Pickfords wanted to know when the sculpture would set sail. She tried to think of someone helpful with a good view of Hong Kong harbour. So she phoned the Harlequin Bar, on top of the Mandarin Oriental hotel.

Helen: Could you please look out of the window and tell me if the Bamboo Man is moving yet?

Barman: I'm sorry madam. Please say again.

Helen: Could you please look out of the window and tell me if the Bamboo Man is moving yet?

Barman: Just a minute madam. I will page him for you.

Pen-pusher: Don't you just hate it when you phone someone who isn't there, and you have to leave a message with someone who is really not interested in helping? Hong Kong food writer Ilona Toth rang the Hong Kong head office of fast food chain Hardee's.

Hardee's: You have to speak to our representative.

Toth: May I speak to him, please?

Hardee's: Not here.
Toth: When will he be back?
Hardee's: Next week.
Toth: Can I leave a message?
Hardee's: Yes. Give me your phone number.
Toth: Five, six, five, double-two, double-two.
Hardee's: Name?
Toth: Ilona. I.L.O.N.A.
He still sounded unsatisfied.
Hardee's: Okay. Wait a minute. I have to get a pen.

Injustice scaled: Got a call from the hospital bed of Griffo the Bear. Intrepid reporter Nick Griffin of Metro News uncovered a story, even though he has been laid up in hospital for 4½ months with pancreas problems.

A nurse arrived to weigh him. The reading was only 50 kilos — way below his proper weight.

She was unflustered.

"This must be the ladies' scales," said the nurse.

She returned with another set shortly afterwards. "This is from a male ward," she explained. On these, he weighed 60 kilos.

So this is Griff's discovery: in Hong Kong, a kilo of male does not weigh the same as a kilo of female.

Most blatant lie by a camera shop for not sticking to its original offer: Sarah Morris of Sheung Wan returned to the Apple Camera Shop in Nathan Road, Kowloon, to pay for a Canon EOS 10 a staff member had quoted at a suspiciously cheap HK$3,000.

"I had recognised him on entering the shop, and he had recognised me immediately too," she told us.

"Sorry. No camera," he told her.

"What? Have you run out of stock?"

"No, they finished make. They no more make this model."

"You're telling me Canon does not make the EOS 10 any more?"

"Canon no make ANY cameras now," he said.

Roll over: Writer Simon Winchester phoned the concierge at the Mandarin Oriental hotel to ask him to buy him a copy of a Beethoven record.

Winchester: Do you know who Beethoven is?
Concierge: No. What room is he in?
Winchester: No, no, he's dead.
Concierge: Oh! We'd better call security!

Real classic: Arrived at work feeling relaxed, after having been regaled with classical music, courtesy of the Mass Transit Railway. We think it was Strauss.

We hope the MTR will tell head office staff the names of the tunes this time.

Last year, during a similar experiment, a friend of ours phoned to ask the name of a piece of music, so she could buy it.

Caller: What is the music that is playing in the stations?
MTR: It's a tape.
Caller: Yes, but what do you call it?
MTR: We call it "a tape".

ONLY IN HONG KONG

The Shining: Nick Gray, a computer consultant at Standard Chartered Bank, was innocently strolling to work.

He spotted a shoe-shine man near Alexandra House in Central Hong Kong and decided that having gleaming shoes would start the week off on the right foot.

The shoe-shine man tut-tutted. "Your sole is coming off. No problem. I fix," he said.

He splashed a large amount of Superglue between the sole and the uppers, and started working on the shoes.

During this, Nick felt a strange, cold, creeping sensation – the Superglue was penetrating his shoe and was soaking into his sock.

The computer man leapt into action, hopping around on one foot trying to get the shoe off. It was stuck fast.

Passengers on nearby buses watched goggle-eyed, commenting to each other about this *gweilo's* laughable attempt at *t'ai chi*.

A horrible vision intruded into Nick's mind. "I am going to be wearing this one shoe for the rest of my life,' he thought. With a superhuman yank, he managed to remove the item of footwear.

Then he began the even tougher task of taking his sock off, while continuing his one-foot pogo dance.

By this time, passers-by were stopping to watch what they thought was a highly skilled breakdance demonstration.

Eventually the sock — now stiff as cardboard — came off.

"After all this, he still charged me," said an amazed Nick. "HK$15 for the shine and HK$15 for the glue."

Well, Nick, you wanted to start the week off on the right foot, and you certainly did that.

Skin-head: Saw some young men strolling through Admiralty with fashionably ragged jackets emblazoned with words such as "Harley Davidson" and "DEATHMETAL".

One chap was walking noticeably apart from the others.

On the back of his battered-looking tough guy denim jacket were the words: "NU SKIN".

Record profits: Rich Surrency of Noble House nipped into Hong Kong Records, the new music shop on the corner of Hutchison House. He saw a boxed set of CDs which he wanted to buy — then he was shocked to notice that it cost far more than in other music stores in Central.

Rich: Why is it so expensive?

(Saleswoman picks up a single CD from a rack nearby and points to the sticker.)

Saleswoman: This CD is HK$90.

Rich: So?

Saleswoman: This CD is available at other stores for HK$60.

Rich: So?

Saleswoman: We are always about 40 per cent more than other stores. It's company policy.

Rich told us afterwards: "This was my first encounter in Hong Kong with an honest saleswoman. Hope she never works for a Nathan Road store."

Tasteless beast: An anthem for Hong Kong's meat and offal industry:

(Chorus:)
All things bright and beautiful
All creatures great and small
All things wise and wonderful
We like to eat them all.
(Verse:)
Each little beast that staggers
Each little bird that sings
We eat their tiny bodies
We eat their little wings
(Repeat chorus.)

Out of order: James Ryan of Mid-Levels got a letter from the Wellcome supermarket's home delivery service.

"Dear Customer,

"We will have our annual dinner on February 22, the placed orders on that day afternoon will be postponed the next day or the day after tomorrow. Therefore, please place your orders three days in advance so as to avoid delay.

"Thank you for your attention."

Well, hope that's perfectly clear to everyone.

Domino effect: The Golden Palette restaurant in Wan Chai was trying to attract diners. As well as new dishes, they added a live band. Steve Elrick of BSB Advertising was sitting there, listening to an original interpretation of *The Girl from Ipanema*.

"All this sterling work at attracting the customers was somewhat let down," said Steve. "This was when, appearing in the entrance for everyone to see, was Domino's Pizza delivery man. It was time for the staff's dinner."

Water logged: A pair of those cinematic masterpieces known as Public Service Announcements burst onto our television screen at 2 am on TVB.

The first vignette, *Wash Your Food*, showed someone washing vegetables under running water. The second, *Save Water*, warned people not to wash things under running water.

No doubt there is a third in the series, called *Waste Taxpayers' Money*.

Fly-by knight: Beauty queen Elaine Sung was standing forlornly waiting for a taxi at the Star Ferry on Kowloon-side. There was not a cab to be had for love nor money.

Suddenly a chap pulled up in a private car and offered her a lift.

"There are no taxis around at all," said the driver, smiling sweetly. "But I'll give you a ride — for HK$100."

Ms Sung declined this unchivalrous offer.

"Okay. Well then, would you like to buy a mobile phone instead?" he said, unperturbed.

"No, thank you," said Elaine.

"Are you in need of any insurance then?"

She again declined. Looking downcast, the failed salesman motored off into the sunset, leaving the dazzling young woman on the kerb.

A classic illustration of the Hong Kong definition of a pervert: "A sexual deviant is a man who prefers women to money."

Modern habit: Lunched at the Viceroy of India in the Sun Hung Kai Centre. At the next table was a Buddhist monk — complete with shaven head, robes, sandals and so on, sitting next to a spiritual-looking woman who looked like an acolyte of some sort.

Strolling past their table on the way to get some more of the Viceroy's multi-coloured poppadoms, we glanced down to see what was lying in the middle of their table: a recent model super-slim mobile phone.

Press control: Trish Hanley of Professional Party Planners was describing a large corporate project to a Hong Kong customer. He seemed satisfied with most aspects of it.

But then he said: "But what do we do about pests?"

Trish was perplexed.

"What if any pests turn up?" he asked. "I'm very concerned about pests."

They had a strange conversation about this at cross-purposes, until she realised that when he said "pests", he meant "the press".

She retraced their steps in the conversation and suddenly it made perfect sense.

Fancy getting so mixed up over what is purely a theoretical distinction!

A close encounter of the very unlucky kind: At about 12.30 pm on Saturday, August 23, 1992, "Ginger" the illegal immigrant heaved himself up to the top of Tai Long Wan and waved to his fellow IIs to follow him.

Coming up the ridge they saw a sturdy-looking *gweilo*.

Ginger, who had a red-blond streak peroxided into his hair, put on his best Cantonese accent.

"*Bin do heui Heung Gong-a?* [Which way to Hong Kong?]," he asked, with an accent that seemed more like Hokkien.

The *gweilo* helpfully pointed in the right direction.

"*Dai lo hai bin do-a?* [Which way to the main road?]," asked Ginger.

The westerner pointed again. A second foreigner, a tall chap, reached the top of the hill and joined them, and shortly afterwards, so did a third.

"*Gor do yau mo gingchat?* [Any cops that way?]," asked Ginger with a glint in his eye.

The *gweilo*, with strained expressions, assured them that there were no police at hand.

The illegal immigrants, delighted with the situation, scampered off to some nearby bushes. There they pulled out some trendy Hong Kong-style gear in which to disguise themselves.

Meanwhile, the three *gweilo* were almost bursting their blood vessels with the strain of trying to keep their faces straight.

The reason? The first was Hong Kong's Secretary for Security, Alistair Asprey, and the other two were his deputies, Ian Strachan and Jim Morris: they were the territory's three most senior individuals in the battle against illegal immigrants.

The three were getting in some practice for the Trailwalker charity walk scheduled for November.

Mr Asprey calmly reached for his mobile telephone and dialled 999.

"Some people have dreadful luck," Mr Strachan commented to his team-mates, as Mr Asprey summoned the border police.

Inconvenience: Don Barwick of Ping Long Village, Tai Po, tells us that the Kowloon-Canton Railway is planning some interesting modifications.

A notice in Tai Wo station informs passengers:

Renovation work is in progress. Toilets will be partially suspended for use.

"I wonder where they are going to suspend them from?" asked Don.

It all sounds a bit arty-farty to us.

More to the point, are ladders going to be supplied?

It could be jolly difficult for old people to use partially suspended toilets!

Low society: Disillusionment hit us in a big way. The Enthusiast Society of Hong Kong (Upper Kwai Chung Village branch in Tsuen Wan) has apparently run out of enthusiasm.

The Enthusiasts were given notice by the Government that they have ceased to exist and are being kicked off the Societies Ordinance.

As this whopping piece of bad news was gazetted on Friday 13 (November 1992), maybe they would like to reform as The Superstitious Society?

Consumer ethic: Simon Cox of Village Road, Happy Valley, was in Toys 'R' Us, when he noticed that all trolleys have signs telling customers not to leave their "personal values in the trolley".

"I make sure I leave all my personal values and scruples safely locked up at home before I go anywhere near the shopkeepers of Kowloon," said Simon.

Disaster movie: Halfway through *Lethal Weapon 3* all the fire alarms went off at the UA Cinema complex in Queensway.

Since the film continued to run, most of the audience decided they would stay where they were. But after 10 minutes, the film stopped — and then the audience decided that something really was wrong, and fled.

One member of the audience, Nikki Sayell of Graffiti restaurant, said that as they moved toward the entrance, they came across proof that everything was normal, or as normal as it could be for Hong Kong.

As the alarms rang and the audience fled, front of house staff were busy selling tickets as fast as they could.

Relatively strange: Clark Pettit, senior information systems analyst at Dow Chemical Pacific, decided to get a supermarket credit card. He applied for a Park'N Shop card for himself and asked for one for his significant other, Beverly Ann. Clark also asked for a supplementary card for their amah, Lily.

He received a reply from Park'N Shop with some bad news in it.

"Dear Customer, we are pleased to advise you that your application for our credit account has been approved with the account number [xxxxxx] being allocated. However, we regret that the supplementary card for your sig. other, Beverly Ann, cannot be issued because it is our policy not to issue supplementary card to anyone other than your immediate relative."

So Clark is entitled to a card, but because he is not actually married to his partner, she is not allowed one.

But in the envelope they found two cards. One for Clark — and one for his AMAH.

At about the same time, Lin Mo-sang of Fanling sent off to Park'N Shop for two cards: one for himself and one for his sister. The reply said: "We regret that the supplementary card for your sister, Lin Yuk-ching, cannot be issued because it is our policy not to issue supplementary card to anyone other than your immediate relative."

So your common law spouse and your siblings are not immediate relatives. Your maid, however, is.

Welcome to Hong Kong family life.

Big problem: Tony Hayman of Mondial Expatriate Services, Great Eagle Centre, was at the counter on the 12th floor of the Hong Kong Government's Department of Agriculture and Fisheries.

His eye strayed to a label on an in-tray which said: "Endangered snakes, hippo, mammoth, plants, etc."

"I couldn't help wondering as to how many mammoth licences are applied for each year," he said. "Correct me if I'm wrong, but it has always been my understanding that mammoths went out of production a few millenia ago."

Clearly they don't update the filing system at the Ag and Fish very often.

Smoking room: Jardines' executives tend to avoid bringing up the topic of the firm's inglorious past as an opium-pusher.

So we were curious to get a call from Hong Kong photographer Hugh Van Es. He had recently passed by a Jardines holiday home near Pui O on Lantau Island, and noticed that it had been named "Pipedream".

Coincidence, surely?

Buyer hands over record on a plate: There was a quintessential Hong Kong moment near the end of the Government's car number plate auction.

Under the hammer was the last registration number. Auctioneers Paul Hart and Nancy Hung had managed to wheedle more than HK$9 million out of the audience.

The last number plate, "119", had been bid up to HK$450,000, and this was clearly the last offer.

The auctioneers did some quick maths. They noticed that the final tally for the whole auction, HK$9.86 million, was close to the record figure achieved at previous car plate auctions, but would not surpass it.

Then Nancy had a brainwave. She asked the final bidder to bid again, HK$10,000 higher than his previous offer, in effect bidding against himself. She explained that this would enable them to break the record.

The zillionaire thought about this for a moment, and then happily complied. As a result he forked out HK$460,000 for the plate, and a new record was set.

This is clear proof that so much money is sloshing around in Hong Kong that you can have some just for the asking.

Bottom Line: John Adams of P & O Containers was browsing in the market in Stanley, Hong Kong, when he found a shop selling garments emblazoned with the words "BUM EQUIPMENT".

Curiously, they are garments designed for the upper body.

Must be a range of export designer garments targeted at American tramps.

Lost in transit: The DA Services group sent a letter to Marylee Kock of Freetime Outdoor Ltd.

"Attention: Personnel Manager," it said.

"We Provide Personnel Recruitment For Your Company.

"Enclosed, please find selected candidate seek position of Junior Secretary in your company."

Whoever she was, she wasn't in the envelope when

Marylee got it. She must have escaped, or perhaps got stuck in a postal sorting machine.

Service charge: At a Battle of Britain thanksgiving service at Sek Kong, the order of service urged that worshippers honour "money" instead of "memory".

The prayer of penitence read as follows: "Almighty and everlasting God, you are always more ready to hear than we to pay."

What's going on? Has yuppyism infiltrated the church in Hong Kong?

Surly bird: Robin Moyer, *Time* magazine man in Hong Kong, commented that the territory's shopkeepers seem to have re-written one of Ben Franklin's sayings for their own use: "Surly to bed, surly to rise."

Word of mouth: Tax consultant Fred Fredricks was in the Foreign Correspondents' Club of Hong Kong, musing over Peggy Lam's suggestion filed in the Legislative Council entitled: "Oral sex as a serious crime."

"It would destroy the sex lives of most of my friends here," Fred said, looking around the bar. "Most of them don't do anything other than talk about it."

Greenish ploy: Raymond Smith, co-boss of Faces restaurant in Citibank Plaza, Hong Kong, had a sudden attack of greenism. He resolved to go to Park'N Shop and buy one of those wonderful environmentally friendly shopping bags, which cost HK$6-odd.

He nipped into the supermarket in Discovery Bay and purchased the said bag.

Staff handed it over — neatly wrapped in a plastic Park'N Shop bag.

Yes, Park'N Shop will save the world from environmental disaster.

Beer money: Oozed into the back of a briefing where San Miguel announced it was sponsoring the Vietnam marathon.

The beer firm handed over the first payment in cash: wads of banknotes stuffed into a giant tankard. Executives from all the groups involved gathered around and clutched the tankard for a group photograph.

"Smile," said the photographer. They looked rather serious.

"Smile," he said again and they produced feeble grimaces.

Then he had an idea.

"Just look at all that money," said the photographer.

The Suits looked at the pile of cash. Their eyes lit up and large, natural grins broke out.

The bulb flashed.

Boss to you: Norman Jones of MotivationAsia phoned Reliance Motors to ask for the name of the managing director.

Jones: May I ask the name of the managing director?
Reliance: No.
Jones: I'm sorry. Could you please tell me the name of the managing director?
Reliance: No.
Jones: What do you mean "no"?
Reliance: I can't tell you.
Jones: Why not? Is it a secret?
Reliance: Yes.

It must be jolly hard to be the managing director of a big company like that if you have to do it all under a secret identity.

Does he hold his board meetings wearing a Batman mask?

Hive of flowers: Jill Lovatt of Two Pacific Place was in The Health Shoppe in Queensway Plaza the other day, looking at their extensive range of honeys.

New Zealand honey was HK$22.50, but a nearby Tasmanian honey had no price on it.

Jill asked the assistant how much the Tasmanian honey was. She looked it up and said: "HK$37.50."

"Why is it so much more than the New Zealand honey?" Jill asked.

"Tasmanian honey from bees," the assistant said solemnly.

"But so is New Zealand honey."

"No. New Zealand honey is from FLOWERS. Tasmanian honey is from BEES," explained the salesgirl, and went off to serve someone else.

Honestly. Some customers don't know anything!

Keep on truckin': Continental Airlines is promoting holidays on the Pacific islands of Saipan and Guam. Kevin Walker, general manager of Jebson Co, Hong Kong, wanted to take advantage of the superb diving on the neighbouring island of Truk. He called the airline.

Walker: Do you also have holidays to Truk?

Continental: You want a holiday in a truck?

Walker: No, we want to go to Truk.

Continental: I am sorry. We only do trips in planes. You can't go by truck.

Walker: No, you don't understand. Truk is the name of an island near to Saipan.

Continental: No. We don't go to Saipan by truck either — goodbye.

Click.

Honestly. Some passengers make the most ridiculous requests!

Man of letters: Anyone interested in fake goods may wish to nip down to The Lanes, which are little alleyways between Queen's Road and Des Voeux Road in Central, Hong Kong.

You will see people selling goods by Moschino. These are distinctive because they have the name in large metal capital letters on the products.

As you approach, you will be surprised to find that the name does not read MOSCHINO, but rather WOSCHINO.

You pick up the handbag and say: "Isn't this supposed to say 'Moschino'?"

The salesman leans forward, shows you his screwdriver, and says: "You buy. I turn 'W' upside-down."

Rough justice: A ticket tout with some tickets for the sold-out Rugby Sevens game walked into the Bull and Bear pub in Central, Hong Kong.

Tout: Anyone want any Rugby Sevens tickets?
Buyer: Yes. How many have you got?
Tout: Eight.
Buyer: How much do you want for them?
Tout: Well, naturally I expect a bit of a premium because of their scarcity value. You pay double the face value.
Buyer: Okay, But can I have a look at them first?
(Tout hands over eight tickets to buyer. Buyer immediately rips them into shreds and sprinkles them on the floor.)
Buyer: That's what I think of ticket scalpers.
(Round of applause from people watching.

What a card: Office estate agent Mark Denny-Fairchild of Queens Property Consultants, Wan Chai, was at the marriage registry at City Hall recently with blushing Thai bride-to-be Marlee Buntham Sridet.

When the time came for the witnesses to do their bit, they were asked to give their ID card numbers or passport numbers. Uh-oh. No identification.

Panic.

A guest, David Barnard of Speedflex, dashed out to the Star Ferry and managed to persuade a pair of tourists from the UK to agree to act as witnesses.

But once he ushered them into the registry, he found that the problem had vanished.

Staff had decided that a Mastercard was acceptable as an ID card for the purposes of a Hong Kong marriage.

Beak condition: Balakrishna Rao of Mansfield Road, the Peak, nipped into Park'N Shop in the Hang Seng Bank building in Central. In the bathroom supplies section was a sign saying "Toothpaste for Chicken".

Now we have nothing against people spoiling their domestic animals. But poultry don't even have teeth.

Least convenient training: Famous Qigong teacher Ji Chen has been offering courses in Lantau island, Hong Kong. Qigong is translated as "Chinese Salusophic Static-Dynamic Therapeutical Exercises for Utilisation of Ethereal Energy".

One technique is "Toilet Qigong". Upon completion of one's natural functions, one should contract and relax the muscles of the organs concerned 36 times.

Least pleasant wait in the world: the ladies' toilet queue at a Qigong convention.

His number's up: Ouch. Hong Kong Investors were much pained this week by a false rumour that Deng Xiaoping had died.

It was widely believed that the fall was engineered by a group of investors who were heavily short on index futures and needed to unload them.

The amazing thing about that incident was that the index paused at 4,444.14 — meaning "dead, dead, dead, dead and surely dead" — as if destiny itself was confirming the rumour.

The inescapable conclusion: God is holding a major short position on Hang Seng Index Futures.

You've seen the show, now visit the place . . . : We have often said that living in Hong Kong is like hanging out in the Twilight Zone.

Well, Shelley Fines was at the Kowloon-Canton Railway station near her home in Tai Wai when an unmistakable sound cut through the air.

Doo-dee-doo-doo, doo-dee-doo-doo, doo-dee-doo-doo . . .

Yes. It was the theme from the classic TV show "The Twilight Zone", a programme in which normal people get thrown into weird supernatural situations.

But you know what's really strange? The fact that it does not seem to have that music played in public places in Hong Kong.

It seems exactly right.

Expressly yours: Tracy Lai of the Kowloon-Canton Railway contacted us to pass on a message to Shelley Fines.

The theme of "The Twilight Zone" is being played at Tai Wai station on a trial basis, to warn dawdling passengers that the doors are about to shut, she said. "Would you like to suggest some other tunes?" Tracy added.

What do you think? We came up with the following:
It's Now or Never

Too Late Baby
Knockin' on Heaven's Door
Take the A Train
Station to Station
The Door to Paradise
Someone's Knockin' on the Door
Ghost Train

Out of touch: Bill Wintrip of Can Ltd, a civil engineering firm in Lippo Centre, Hong Kong, specialising in difficult access jobs, had a problem with his mobile phone.

He took it into CSL's highly efficient Mobile Customer Care Centre in Wan Chai for a quick repair.

The helpful girl at the reception told him to leave it with them and the repair would take about four hours.

"What time should I come back for it?" asked Bill.

"No problem, sir, I will phone you when it's ready," she said.

"But..."

Omnivorous: Dorothy Brown of the Omni group's Hong Kong Hotel got a letter from a Mr Okunoye Sunday of Lagos, Nigeria.

Mr Sunday writes: "I want you to send me special gifts, sir, such as: T-shirt, soap, tie, clip-tie, pen, shampoo, body lotion, shower cap, hair conditioner, chocolate, toys, Dettol, tea, sugar, perfume, shaving blade, shoe polish, toothbrush and paste, matches, sticker, postcard, sewing kits, spoon, knife, fork, keyholder, balloon, belt and bath foam."

We can only assume that Mr Sunday is planning to open his own hotel in Nigeria. There must be easier ways to acquire supplies.

Clear as Mudd: Margaret, wife of Mui Wo engineer Don

Mudd, phoned the Hong Kong office of Bank of Tokyo to ask for some information.

"Yes," said the receptionist. "What is your name?"

"Who wants to know?" asked Margaret.

The receptionist said: "Well, Mrs Whowantstoknow, if you would ring 862 ... "

Tangled words: The language of China Club boss David Tang can become fruity when he gets excited. He phoned a businessman the other day.

Tang: Can I speak to Mr Lee?
First Voice: What is your name?
Tang: Tang.
First Voice: How to spell?
Tang: T.A.N.G.
First Voice: Okay. (Click.)
Second Voice: Hello?
Tang: Can I speak to Mr Lee?
Second Voice: What is your name?
Tang: Tang.
Second Voice: How to spell?
Tang: T.A.N.G.
Second Voice: Okay. (Click.)
Third Voice: Hello?
Tang: Can I speak to Mr Lee?
Third Voice: What is your name?
Tang: Tang.
Third Voice: How to spell?
Tang: T.A.N.G.
Third Voice: Which company?
Tang: A f***ing good company.
Third Voice: How to spell?
Tang: F ...

Decline and fall: Ken Gibbons of Pacific View, Tai Tam Road, often has trouble communicating his surname. He phoned a friend at Peat Marwick recently.

Receptionist: Good morning. Can I help you?
Ken: Yes, please may I speak to Mr Bond?
Receptionist: Yes, who's calling?
Ken: Mr Gibbons.
Receptionist: Could you spell that please?
Ken: Yes. G.I.B.B.O.N.S.
Receptionist: Mr Giv —
Ken: No, Mr GIBBONS, with two Bs, as in Bye Bye.
Receptionist: Bye bye!
Click.

THE AVERAGE ASIAN'S ATTENTION SPAN IS SO SHORT THESE DAYS THAT HE FREQUENTLY STARTS A SENTENCE BUT FORGETS TO

I was horrified to read in a survey recently that a relaxed man will think about the opposite sex approximately once every 75 seconds.

I find this extremely difficult to believe. Everyone knows men are fundamentally unfrivolous creatures, with a far higher degree of concentration than members of competing genders, such as female. Topics on which the typical male enjoys pondering, include, well, things such as . . .

Hmm? Sorry. Lost my train of thought. Anyway, I utterly refute the nonsensical allegation that every time a man tries to focus on something for more than a minute, his mind wanders off and he begins to . . .

So. Right then. What were we talking about? Oh yes, the male attention span. Take me for example. I can single-mindedly latch onto a subject and stick to it with all the tenacity of a sucker-fish using super-glue for lipsalve.

The Football Association cup was a bit dull this year,

wasn't it? And what about that fellow Neil Armstrong, walking on the moon in 1969?

But I digress. Back to the survey. For me, the most distressing thing was the finding that three out of four readers will not read a magazine article or an essay in a non-fiction book all the way to the end. Most just scan a third of it.

This means the chances are that you — that's right, I'm talking to YOU READING THIS NOW, SO DON'T TRY TO COME OVER ALL INNOCENT — are at this precise nano-second wondering whether to go off and do something more enjoyable, such as having a double root canal without anaesthetic.

If it is true that attention spans are getting shorter, my friend Chris is in trouble. He works for the pay-as-you-listen telephone industry, which is just taking root in Asia. The caller (known in telecommunications jargon as "Old Muggins" or "the Dork-Brain") pays up to US$1 per minute, so they want to hold his attention as long as possible.

The way to hold the Dork-Brain's attention, says Chris, is to start with an enticing message promising something at the end of the tape. Example:

Opening remark: "Thank you for calling Cheeky Charlotte's Storyline. If you listen right to the end, I'll tell you something personal about you and me."

(Ten minutes of random musings follow.) Closing remark: "Here's the personal bit about you and me: you've just wasted a ton of money on me. Ha ha ha. Tough luck, sucker."

Some people say attention spans will be shortened by the arrival of MTV in Asia. MTV, short for "empty TV", is a channel of high-speed pop music images.

Imagine an MTV-satiated scholar going to a bookshop. "I'd like to buy *One League Under The Sea* by Jules Verne, please."

Bookseller: "You mean *20,000 Leagues?*"

Scholar: "No time, dude; just hit me with one."

Am I being alarmist? No. I have noticed a marked increase recently of young people afflicted with "Someone Better Syndrome". This is when you talk to a person at a party and they keep looking over your shoulder to see if there's someone better in the room.

This has happened to me after I have been regaling a member of the opposite sex with fascinating reminiscences of my life for as little as two hours.

Anyway, I quite like the telephone man's idea, so I shall adopt it. Anyone who reads right to the end of this article will read something deeply personal about you and me.

Oh. We are already at the end, are we? Okay, so here it is. You have now read more of this article than even my wife, a discriminating reader who refused to give more than a cursory glance at the first third of it. At least one of my readers has a bit of taste.

Now what was that nice daydream I was having before I started this . . .?

A SERIOUS WARNING ABOUT A GRAVE DANGER WE ARE ALL IN

I have an urgent message to all caring, sensitive old-fashioned people. The time has come for us to BLEEEEEEP. Sorry, that wasn't me: that was the paging device of the chap at the next table. What I am saying is that the hour has come for us all to stand up and BLEAT-BLEAT. BLEAT-BLEAT. Blast it. That's the waiter's mobile phone. Let's have this conversation in a quieter place, such as the building site next door.

Right. Much better. What I have to say can best be illustrated by telling you about the incident that alerted me to the grave danger we are in.

A Malaysian friend of mine, who has been working in Tokyo, arrived in Hong Kong a month ago. The airline, just for the fun of it, sent his suitcases to an uninhabited atoll in the Pacific. He had to borrow clothes from his host, to save himself from the abject disgrace of wearing the same designer belt two days in a row.

But this is the weird bit. Every single borrowed item — right down to the underwear (Calvin Klein) and the bathrobe (ex-Mandarin Oriental) — was EXACTLY the same brand as the stuff in his suitcase.

These chaps were not related, yet they dressed like supernaturally-linked twins in corny American movies.

Coincidence? That day I started a concerted program of peering down the necks of my friends' clothing to spot designer labels.

Within three weeks I had come to two shocking realisations. One was that women did not like me peering down their necklines.

The second was that this "same-brand" phenomenon applies internationally to the entire sub-culture of people known as suits, yuppies, high achievers, dinks, and so on. Be they from Labuan or London, Manila or Manhattan — they dress the same, talk the same, and fill their apartments with the same toys. They all own at least one album by Dire Straits, and one classical album, which is always Vivaldi's *Four Seasons.*

It is not that they have the same taste. There can be only one conclusion. It is because . . . it is SOME SORT OF UNIFORM.

They are plotting something.

It is horrifying, but can you ignore evidence this comprehensive? After having discussed this at length with my mentor/bartender, I have pieced together the outline of what I am now almost sure they are scheming.

1. At some secret, pre-arranged signal, the Suits will make a concerted bid for world domination. They will achieve this through their already considerable influence in global financial manipulation. The planet Earth will be renamed Yuptopia 1.

2. Non-yuppies will be herded into camps at sea level (the

Lowlands) and the Yuppies will congregate, guffawing over cocktails, on higher grounds (the Yuplands). The non-yups will be set to work making small, useless electronic gadgets in black leather pouches under a working philosophy known as Yuptilitarianism.

3. The wearing of any non-designer garment (that is, any item costing less than US$500) or any wristwatch costing less than US$1,000 will be punishable by death.

4. A shrine will be set up in the middle of each city, and adherents will file past, chanting the yuppie mantra: "Rolex; Filofax; Porsche cars; heart attacks."

Once this basic stage of the takeover is complete, and Yuptopia has been established, life will settle down a bit. Over the following few years, a delegation of yuppie lawyers (known as LawSuits) will pass legislation to re-fashion modern society in their image. Without going into detail, here are a few basic points to give you the flavour of what they are plotting:

(a) The whole structure of working life will be altered. Payrises will be awarded to employees who take the longest and most expensive lunches. A bonus will be paid to anyone who completely fails to return from lunch on a given day.

(b) For a few years, no conversation will be allowed except through mobile phones, to encourage their use. This applies to all forms of communication, including "pillow talk" between co-habitees, and the cooing-and-gurgling repartee favoured by mothers and babies.

(c) All non-designed items (such as rocks, trees, swamps, etc) will be thrown into the sea and replaced by similar items designed by named designers, who must be Italian and whose names must end in -ucci.

(d) All vehicular transport will be phased out, except for sports cars. All sports cars will be red, because yuppies think red ones go faster.

Oh, I know you think that I am exaggerating, but the signs of the forthcoming revolution are everywhere. What can we do to stop the menace from progressing further?

We need to band together and legislate against them. We need to BLEAT-BLEAT. BLEAT-BLEAT. What's that? The unmistakable sound of a portable phone. One of THEM must be in the vicinity! Whose pocket is the sound coming from?

Oh. It's yours, is it?

WE HAND OUT SOME AWARDS

Worst named information service: When lost in Shanghai, phone 320 0200, and you get a help-line service featuring female operators known collectively as "Miss Information."

Most naive big spender: A family from Taikoo Shing, Hong Kong, who emigrated to Canada, got a phone bill for HK$40,000 after only six weeks.

The trans-Pacific calls had been made by their 10-year-old daughter to school friends in Hong Kong. They confronted her with the fact that she was about to bankrupt them.

"Don't be silly mummy," she replied. "Everyone knows that Hong Kong telephone calls are free."

Best recent administrative decision: This title must go to Singapore for making chewing gum illegal. "Up to now, users were openly chewing in public," an investment manager told us. "Whipped into a frenzy by the spearmint flavour, Singaporeans would do outrageous things, like attempt to think for themselves."

A fund manager claimed to have secret information about the next piece of legislation in the pipeline in the world's cleanest society.

"They are going to make nose-blowing illegal. All foreigners will have to blow their noses one last time at Changi airport on the way in."

Flashiest ID: The world's richest man, the Sultan of Brunei, nipped into a clothes shop in New York in 1991 to make a small purchase: 40 shirts, six pairs of jodhpurs and so on.

The bill was an almost imperceptible US$2,000. The shop assistant, to whom the sultan was just another Asian, demanded identification.

His Richness did not have any. He had not encountered this request before.

A retainer coughed and reached into his wallet.

"Will this do?" he asked, holding up a banknote featuring the shopper. It did.

Least appetising soup: The menu for Noble House restaurant in Central, Hong Kong, offers "Bird's Nest in Sweat Soup (Hot)" for HK$150.

The thought makes us break out in perspiration (cold).

Best Russian restaurant: One recently appeared in Lan Kwai Fong, Hong Kong, called Yelts Inn. Staff have gone out of their way to go for an authentic Russian experience, and the place has been decorated with authenticity.

More or less everything is ready to run at the Yelts Inn — except they don't have a kitchen or a chef, so no food is available, however long you wait.

Yes, that's realism.

Least enticing medicine: A fad is growing in Taiwan and Japan for drinking one's own urine as a cure for arthritis, diabetes, heart disease and cancer.

"Drink the urine first released in the morning as soon as it is gathered," said the *China Times* of Taipei.

The Taiwanese like it with ice.

A report in the *China Post* of Taipei said:

"Local people who have tasted their own urine told the newspaper that it is similar to beer. However, they said that they had not seen any improvement in their health."

Best security plan: PR boss Frank Murdoch was intrigued by the news that the Hong Kong authorities were buying large numbers of cardboard policemen.

"They can catch the robbers who steal fake jewellery brandishing toy guns," he said.

Most memorable example of Hong Kong customer service: Walter Cheung, PR manager for Digital Equipment Corp, shopped at Jusco, a Japanese-run department store in Taikoo Shing, Hong Kong.

The cashier handed him a "customer opinion form" to fill in. The store is holding a campaign to improve standards of customer service.

He did not have a pen. So he went up to the service counter on the ground floor, waved his form and asked to borrow a pen to fill it in with.

Staff member: "NO."

Black death: The Hong Kong Pest Control Association is to give out a new safety award, according to an announcement sent in by David Morgan of Rentokil Hong Kong.

It says the prize will be "HK$10,000 and a plague".

We suppose it is a prize that fits the contest, although we would not fancy it ourselves.

Most shocking survey result: Researchers working for the *Far Eastern Economic Review* asked people in Hong Kong who decided where to put their money.

Fifty-seven per cent of married men in Hong Kong said they, the menfolk, made the decisions. Seventy per cent of married women were equally firm that the decisions were made jointly by both sexes.

Thus 13 per cent of married people in Hong Kong are being fooled in money matters by their spouses.

This is an absolutely shocking finding. Can it really be only 13 per cent?

Best Baby Toy: Want to turn your baby into a rich, spoilt brat? Buy him his own compact disc player. A Japanese-made CD system specially designed for very small children is stocked by Kalms gift shop in Hong Kong for HK$1,750.

It comes in red, green and white plastic, and has a cartoon kitten and the words "Hello Kitty" emblazoned on the front.

When Lai See was a child, we were given a mango stone to play with and we were pitifully grateful.

Best active holiday: Beijing will hold a "Sound of Peace shooting competition with Chinese military weapons", we read in *Bei Fang* magazine.

Boom. Pow. Bang-bang-bang-bang-bang! Yes, you can really get into those Sounds of Peace.

Best toy for Asian yuplets and yuplettes: Hong Kong firm STD Electronics has produced an educational toy to teach children where money comes from: automatic teller machines. My Bank Teller and My Bank Teller Junior are battery operated and come with their own money-card.

Most unusual Christmas card: We got one in January, 1992 signed — well, typed — with the name Leung Wah-chai, chairman of Yanion International Holdings in Hong Kong.

"Wishing you a happy holiday seasoning," was the message.

It was surely the first corporate Christmas card targeted at turkeys.

Rudest letter: Denise Davies of Stanley got a letter from her insurers, Arboretum Brokers (Hong Kong) of Causeway Bay, Hong Kong.

The company has carried out her instructions concerning her houseowners policy, says the letter. "We will be far from happy if we can look after your other insurance needs as well," it added.

Tastiest dish, though often fatty: Japanese gourmets continue to push back the frontiers of culinary science. Hong Kong businessman Peter Rischl saw this on the menu board at the fast food restaurant in the Hong Kong branch of Seibu department store:

Hot European: HK$15.

Lot of them about in Asia these days.

Easiest rule: Quote from rule number one of the official articles of the Hong Kong Computer Society: "A member of the Hong Kong Computer Society . . . will at times exercise competence at least to the level he claims."

Airiest heads: Air China inflight magazine features a behind-the-scenes look at life at CAAC: "To many Chinese, the life of the CAAC staff, especially the cultural life they have in their spare time, seems to be a mystery."

To say nothing of what they do at work.

Best stadium design: The plans for the new Hong Kong Government stadium specify that the thing should be built with "Pre-Cast Vomitory Walls", we heard from Heiko Fenster of Swiss-Sure Co, who has been studying the paperwork.

"The architects are from St Louis, but they seem to know exactly for what distinguished event the stadium is being rebuilt," commented Heiko. "The vomitory walls show that they have been sufficiently briefed on the Rugby Sevens."

It will also be useful if that Mr Bush visits.

Most intriguing caption: In the inflight magazine for Thai Airways' domestic service is a picture of guardsmen marching in formation with the caption: "This year's suspicious moment for the Royal Guards arrives."

Although we have long been interested in Asian mystical sciences, we had never realised that each 12-month period contains a "suspicious moment", but now it has been mentioned, we can think of many.

Most needed civil rights group: We heard of a secret plan among Hong Kong people to form a grassroots organisation to fight silly rules which are spoiling the image of Southeast Asian countries.

Example: the HK$5,000 fine for going "boing" with your subway ticket in Hong Kong.

"A crowd of us are going to get on to the Mass Transit Railway and flick our tickets, unashamedly making a 'boing boing boing' sound," a spokesman said.

Then they are going to fly to Singapore and chew gum in broad daylight.

What if they arrest you and throw you in jail?

"We are talking about civil liberties here. Some things are worth suffering for," vowed the spokesman, his voice brimming with emotion.

Shortest long-haul: Cathay Pacific Airways is running advertisements in Vietnam business publications which say: "Cathay Pacific is proud to announce the only non-stop services from Ho Chi Minh City and Hanoi to Hong Kong."

Non-stop? The implication is that other airlines offer the same route, but have to make refuelling stops on tiny rocky outcrops in the Gulf of Tongkin. Cheeky.

Most demoralised answerphone: Stephanie Busse of the Holiday Inn Worldwide offices in the China Hong Kong City complex, Tsim Sha Tsui, tried to contact the Hong Kong Inland Revenue for two days.

This is what has happened every time:

Answering machine: "I'm sorry but the lines are busy. Please hold on until we answer your call."

(Typical hold music plays for about one minute.)

Answering machine: "I'm sorry but the lines are still busy. Please call again. Bye-bye."

Then the machine hangs up.

Most movable feast: A customer sent in a brochure from the Hong Kong Convention and Exhibition Centre, promoting its Christmas programme.

"A favourite entree at the HKCEC is fresh goose live," it says.

How do they persuade it to stay in front of you while you are eating it? Do they tie it to your plate? Angry geese are not easy to handle, you know.

Holiest Chapel: The charming Bonnie Wu of Ernst and Young Hong Kong wrote to our colleague Chris Chapel. She reverentially addressed the envelope to "Christ Chapel".
Inside was a message: "Dear Christ, Season's Greetings."
Surely it should have said: "Happy Birthday"?

Festive secret: Hong Kong Tax consultant Fred Fredricks got a fax from Baker and McKenzie's Chicago office:
"Privacy and Confidentiality Notice.
"The information contained in this communication is confidential and may be legally privileged. It is intended solely for the use of the individual or entity to whom it is addressed and others authorised to receive it. If you are not the intended recipient, you are hereby notified that any disclosure, copying, distribution or taking of any action in reliance on the contents of this information is strictly prohibited."
This incredibly secret information consisted of two messages:
(a) The office will be closed for the Christmas Holiday.
(b) Have a happy holiday and joyous new year.

Hate and hearty: Most colourful Christmas greeting received this year came from eccentric former Hong Kong auxiliary policeman Yaqub Khan.
This is his usual fax jam-packed with violent, passionate invective against the establishment. The typed page is filled with phrases such as "British traitor racist colonial dirty rotten scums".
Then there is a handwritten addition at the bottom. "A Merry Christmas and a Happy New Year. May all your wishes come true for 1993. With warm regards, Yaqub Khan."

WHY MEN DON'T HAVE ABDOMENS

BOFFINS recently published some apparently epoch-making research papers suggesting that men and women think in quite different ways. Members of the two sexes even speak with separate vocabularies, they discovered.

Well done, scientists. Welcome to Planet Earth.

Honestly, you have to feel sorry for research fellows. They spend years and years finding out what the rest of us already know.

To reach these conclusions, fact-finders with clipboards spent months analysing transcripts of conversations, and making charts of words frequently used by women, but not men, and vice versa.

It apparently never occurred to these (mainly male) researchers that they could check out their hypotheses quickly and simply through a time-saving but rather dangerous experiment, known as Talking To A Woman.

On behalf of readers of this publication, I decided to

check out the findings through fearless practical experimentation.

Hypothesis One: Men and women and women use entirely different words for body parts, even when both of them have the same part at the same location.

Example: words for the midriff. If you are a woman, you have an "abdomen" or a "tummy". If you are a man, you have a "belly" or "guts".

I watched my entire library of Arnold Schwarzenegger videos. Amazing to relate, Arnie NEVER once said: "Damn! They got me in the abdomen," or "I gotta conviction that he's alive. I feel it in my tum-tum."

On the other hand, the aerobics teacher on my wife's exercise videos spoke endlessly about abdominal scrunches, but not once did she say to her audience: "Belly in. Belly out. You can do it. Don't you want to have nice-looking guts?"

Hypothesis Two: Girls are better at forming complex sentences than boys.

One of my sister's little girls once made a jam sandwich in the kitchen, and made a long speech about it, which went something like this: "Mummy sayth I'm a vewy good lickle girl 'cos I know how to make myself a samwidge and I know how to clean up the kitchen afterwardth and I'm nearly five and half and this is my dolly who is called Emma and she's gonna help me eat the samwidge . . ." etc, etc.

Long before she had finished speaking, the sandwich in question had been summarily inhaled by a small boy belonging to a visitor. I noted that the only aural expression of his feelings he had made during his entire visit had been preternaturally noisy expulsions of air from unlikely parts of his body.

Hypothesis Three: Males have an ability to conceptualise in spatial terms which females lack.

It struck me that this is a scientific basis for those cruel jokes that chauvinists make about women drivers not being able to reverse into parking spaces.

One cannot help but marvel at the wonders of evolution. Thousands of years before cars had been invented, Mother Nature knew men were going to be obsessed with them. This bit of male brain can now be thought of as the Reverse Parking Nodule.

Hypothesis Four: A woman has a proportionately larger corpus callosum.

Actually, this is one the things that first attracted me to my wife. She has a remarkably well-turned corpus callosum.

Readers I'm sure know that the corpus callosum is the fibrous bridge that links the right hand (abstract) part of the brain with the left hand (logical) part.

She and I continually talk at cross purposes because I am talking from my left half while she has the ability to wander in and out of the right hand side.

Hypothesis Five: Men have almost no concept about what they look like. This explains why balding men, such as your present narrator, desperately try to disguise their cranial shortcomings with bizarre headgear. We fool ourselves into thinking it takes attention away from the tops of our heads, until some woman with a bulbous corpus callosum informs us that the opposite is true.

Hypothesis Six: Most men who watch a television show for the first time cannot remember any music attached to it. But many women can actually hum the theme music.

Again, this can only be ascribed to the wonders of evolution. Somehow, that wonderful DNA molecule knew that 70 per cent of the homo sapians who would watch TV soap operas after the TV had been invented would be women. No doubt scientists will classify this part of a woman's brain as the Soap Opera Homing Device Nodule.

I know these facts are true, even without scientific data.

I've got a gut feeling about them.
And I don't mean an abdomen feeling.

MISDIRECTED MALE

TODAY, we are going to discuss that oft-debated question of health: just how beneficial is it to sleep with industrial machinery?

But just before getting down to this controversial issue, we interrupt this article to make room for a plea from a reader, whom we shall call Ms X (not her real name). Ms X wants to know if anyone has the answer to a question which has bothered her for years: where are all the men?

Surveys continually point out that more men are born then women. The most recent figures from the United Nations say that there are 35,904,000 more men than women in the world, or 35,903,999, not counting the pop singer Prince.

Although the surplus of male babies is evident worldwide, it is most pronounced in Asia, where boy-children are openly favoured.

"But when you want to marry one, you can't find one for love nor money," moaned Singapore-born Ms X (who has tried both).

Take Hong Kong for example. There are 5,822,500 people in the territory, of which 2,854,200 are women and 2,968,300 men.

This means that there are 114,100 lonely men in this city who don't have a female partner and will *never* be able to get one, because there aren't enough to go round.

Who is going to break the bad news to these poor chaps? Certainly not me. I suggest the Government write each of them a letter in a plain brown envelope.

You may think it is not possible to pick out which males will be left behind.

But it is. Ms X has a cunning plan to pinpoint these chaps and isolate them in one place. The scheme is called: Ms X's 1993 All-Hong Kong Folk Dance World Record Attempt.

She wants to get everyone in Hong Kong to go to Victoria Park and do a folk dance step called the doe-see-doe. Instructions:

(a) The men stand on one side.
(b) The women stand on the other.
(c) The men and women hold hands.
(d) The men and women mince about a bit.

And what will emerge at the end of the line, stretching out into Causeway Bay? Yes: a queue of 114,100 mortified and embarrassed men who don't have partners.

Even if a percentage of these are partnerless for good reason (for instance, they may have nasal hair, funny moustaches, an incorrect number of heads, or they may be Prince, etc), we are still talking about tens of thousands of marriageable men.

What will Ms X do with the leftovers? Send them to Italy. There are 328,000 marriageable spare women in Italy, largely because of the Italian male pastime of blowing up each other's cars with landmines.

There is some advice we can give to these lonely Italian women. First, they should head to their local industrial machinery shop, and buy a magnet.

Scientists have discovered that people should, ideally, sleep with a powerful magnet strapped to the crown of their heads. Ask your shopkeeper for a magnet of at least 3,950-guass in strength. A US physician called Dr William Philpott has found that it gives you better skin tone, makes you feel and look younger, and generally improves your contribution in romantic matters.

Of course, people may wonder why you take a can of Three-In-One industrial grease to bed with you. But they'll laugh on the other side of their wrinkled faces when you look like Dorian Gray, while they look like his portrait after it has been dry-cleaned by my local drycleaner.

Looking back over what I have written, I have realised that this whole article may be deeply worrying for shy, single men, especially in Hong Kong.

Well let me reassure you. The male surplus in Hong Kong has dropped by slightly over 50 per cent in the past 10 years. That means that by the year 2000, there should be exactly the same number of men and women.

The whole territory will become one giant happy doe-see-doe.

If the trend continues on the same lines after that, there will actually be some surplus women knocking around, and men are advised to look their best so as to be ready for that coming golden age.

I have to go now. I have to get to the industrial machinery shop before it closes.

HITLER WONG AND THE HUNG FAT BRASSIERE CO

Visitors to Hong Kong are always stunned by the names chosen by individuals and companies here. The most common names include Lee, Choo, Kee, Tung and Tak. These are innocent enough as single syllables, but put them together, translate into English and you end with some unique names:

The territory has a shop called Tack Kee Plastic Watch Company. You'll find a medicine shop called Au-Choo. You'll find a company offering motor boats called the Lee Kee Motor Boat Service. We also have the Hung Fat Brassiere Company. And Harry Rolnick tells us that there is a temple on one of the islands called the Sher Lee Temple.

The staff of the companies often have even stranger names. Hong Kong people like to make sure they are remembered, so they adopt unusual foreign names, such as Nausea Yip (a secretary) and Pubic Ha (an employee on a girlie magazine).

Dan Lavelle tells us that the Hyatt hotel group employs a concierge named "Handsome Tung." He is not just a pretty face.

Stroll past the Police Officers' Club in Hong Kong, and you may find your ears assaulted by the phrase: "Christ! I need a drink." Don't be too shocked. It is not that a member of the police is committing blasphemy. The barman's name is Christ Wong.

When Lai See held a contest for unusual namecards, the wackiest ones were unprintable in a family newspaper. "Long Dick" is a fairly common boy's name. Two young women had name cards revealing their first names to be "Vagina", and we had one Pudenda.

The common Chinese surname "Shit" is now usually written "Sit", although in 1993 there were still nine Shits in the residential phone directory, so to speak. These included two people called Shit Man Wai, one Shit Mi Ying, one Shit Yiu Sang and one Shit Lot Tai.

But it isn't just Orientals who have odd names. I have a very good friend in Hong Kong whose family name is Howley. In Hawaii, the word hoale is a bad word for foreigner. It is much nastier than the word "gweilo". Hoale means 'stupid bloody foreigner'.

Anyway, when Ms Joan Howley went to Hawaii, the staff at the immigration desk were amazed at her name.

"Look," they said. "Here's a stupid bloody foreigner whose actual NAME is stupid bloody foreigner."

Every time this columnist meets someone at a party this happens:

Them: What's your name?
Us: Nury.
Them: Nice to meet you, Uri.
Us: Not Uri. Nury. With an 'N'.
Them (aside to spouse): Good lord, dear, there's a chap

here called Urine.

Too polite: The assistant operations manager at JAS Forwarding HK of Kowloon Bay is a gentleman named "Thankie Yue", we hear from Tom Marrin of the Royal Trading Corp.

Can you imagine concluding a business deal with him?
Customer: Well, thanks very much. And what did you say your name was?
Yue: Thankie Yue.
Customer: No, thank YOU. But what was your name?
Yue: Thankie Yue.
Customer: Really, it was my pleasure. Are you going to tell me your name?
Yue: Thankie Yue.
Etc, etc.

You too, huh: Got a note from a Hong Kong businessman who supplied his name but did not want it in print, presumably out of guilt.

"I knew a girl who worked in Beijing for an American consultancy firm. Her name was Tinga Horny," he said.

She always introduced herself by saying: "Hi. I'm Horny."

The replies were always the same.
"So am I."

Right note: China's cabinet recently proposed joining a world convention protecting copyright on music.

The man with the responsibility for the job is a Mr Song. True.

In good taste: Bob Rossi of Tru (HK) tells us that there is a bank teller at Citibank in the Hankow Centre, Hong Kong, by the name of Candy Man.

He also met a shipping clerk called Lemon Chu.

Hope they never go to Singapore. Candy Man would probably find herself banned from the Lion City's schools, while Lemon Chu probably wouldn't get past immigration.

Pray tell: Reuters Hong Kong has acquired a sales manager called Mantis Lau.

Does that mean that if sales are not going too well, he will be a praying Mantis?

Coffee's stall: Why do diners at the dai pai dong in Cheung Chau call out: "Coffee, Coffee"?

Because the restaurateur's name is Coffee Leung.

Wonder if he is related to Creamie Leung of Poway Travel or Milk Lam of Mount Parker House? The three of them could start a coffee shop. Let's face it, they could BE a coffee shop.

Doreen Ho of Asia Fair Consultants came across a rising star at TVB called Noodlehead.

In the Bible Belt of the United States, there was a girl called Pinkie Bottom and another one called Etta Turnipseed.

Pussy's in the well: The deputy director of Guangdong Posts and Telecoms bureau is a Mr Ding Dong Hwa, we hear. A very suitable name for a telephone man.

If he should marry a relation of David Bell, would their first child be called Ding Dong Bell?

Heil Wong: You won't insult the sales engineer at Nippon-Hon Liftruck of Sham Shui Po by calling him "a little Hitler".

Mariko Tai of Bryanko Textiles showed us his name

card, which proudly reveals that he revels in the name Hitler Wong.

Fast Mover: The information systems manager at Jardine Systems is a Ms Busy Chung. Imagine meeting her:
 "Hi. Who are you?"
 "I'm Busy."
 "Be like that."

Mankind: Ivan Theodoulou of Corporate Communications was surprised to see a staff member at Kentucky Fried Chicken in D'Aguilar Street with the name badge "He-Man."
 "She wasn't," he said.

McNames: The McDonald's in Tsim Sha Tsui seems to be an industry leader in fast food workers with wacky names, according to Doreen Ho of Mei Kang Tang.
 There are staff there called Incredible, Normal, and Army.
 Then she noticed a girl called Execute.
 "Why? Do you know what it means?" asked Doreen.
 "Of course," Execute replied. "Ever since I was a small baby, everyone said I was cute."

Loaves and fish: In the Jack-In-The-Box, an eatery on Cameron Road, Kowloon, there is a sign saying: Employee of the month: Resurrection de Jesus."
 We find this rather difficult to believe.
 If Jesus Christ really came back to earth, would he go for a job selling fast food in Tsim Sha tsui?

Asexual symbol: Ken Davey of Discovery Bay was chortling over the decision by pop singer Prince that he now wants to be known as the male symbol and female symbol combined.

"My guess is that he wants to be recognised as a sex symbol. The trouble is, he can't make up his mind which one," said Ken.

Has Prince thought this through? The obvious problem is that he (or does he prefer "it"?) is going to suffer an amazing worldwide slump in record sales.

Record buyer: I'd like to buy the latest album by, er, you know, er, wotsisname, er . . .

Seller: What are you pointing at?

Record buyer: I'm not pointing. I'm drawing the double-symbol thing he uses as a name. Er, look, why don't you just give me a Kylie Minogue album instead?

Ken also told us about a friend of his who was in a car accident in a residential street in the UK. Two families, the Smiths and a Mr and Mrs Ball, came to his rescue. "Fortunately he was dragged out by the Smiths," said Ken.

Creative types: Got talking to a gentleman in the telephone sales business, who is constantly phoning around Hong Kong. He keeps coming across thought-provoking names that the territory's creative younger generation keeps awarding themselves.

A selection from his list:

Eagle Cheung, Money Lin; Spacey Liang; Anchor Hung; Bilin Yu (she would make a good accountant); Mountain Wang (a big guy); Twinkie To; Anorak Chen; Willy Pong (oops); Piano Chow; Alien Lee; Biggie Yang (show off); Civic de Tsai; Saint Peng; Sicky Tam; Chocolate Lin; Green Show; Ivan Ho; Midas Wu and Vein Shen.

The most baffling on his list is a gentleman called Benweird Ma.

Open sesame: Poke your head around the door of the Mandarin Oriental Cake Shop in Hong Kong and say: "Are you open?"

"Yes," the shop assistant will reply. Even if it is closed.

So would you if your name was Open Wong.

Hi, Ho: Brian Cuthbertson passed on a business card for our memorable names collection. The regional circulation controller of *Action Asia* magazine is Hayde Ho.

We recall getting a fax from someone at Jebsen's PR called Fanny Sit, which reminded us of the delightful Orphelia Kok, also a Hong Kong resident.

Occupants of Fairview Court recently received a letter from Liu Chong Hing Property Management and Agency Co signed by manager Wanky Cheng.

Last but not least, we were interested to see that the director general of Vietnam Airlines is a Mr Nguyen. Nguyen, a common Vietnamese family name, is pronounced "Wing".

One of the herd: Chris Wood of Starflag Shipping met a Taiwanese businessman named Buffalo Lee, and his girlfriend Shu Ting Yu. "A most intimidating couple," he said.

What a load of: Items of junk mail have been arriving on desks all over Asia from Kuala Lumpur firm *World Publications Directory*. This must have the least attractive address in Asia: Mega Mandung Street.

Any Kuala Lumpun readers know the story behind this name?

Hold on a sec. Now do we really want to know?

Dead end job: Eddie Naylor has just come back to Hong Kong from visiting his former home, the village of Bildeston in Suffolk. The following services are provided in the vil-

lage:
> Hardware: Chandler & Son.
> Food and Provisions: Staples.
> Undertaker: Death and Son.

Pulling power: Lawyer Paul Brennock tells us that there is a gentleman working in Hong Kong for Avis Rent-a-Car whose given Chinese name is To Bar.

"One hopes his main occupation does not consist of shunting cars around the Avis compound," said Paul.

His boss would forever be saying: "Get the tow-bar, To Bar."

Urban spaceman: Urban Lehner, editor of the *Asian Wall Street Journal,* is used to people like us making fun of his name.

But nothing prepared him for what he found when he was assigned to Japan, where "Urban" refers to a lifestyle craze.

He found that the train he was on from Nagoya was the "Urban Liner". He mused on a possible headline: "Urban Lehner Rides Urban Liner".

His contacts were wearing pseudo-Italian fashion called "D'Urban", working in the "Urban Elegance" building, and driving Mazda cars called "Urban Break". They read *Urb* magazine while munching food from the Hitachi "Urban Wide 400" fridge.

He was pleased to see a real estate complex described as "Nice Urban".

"Finally, a country where people really understand the importance of being Urban," said Urban.

Born lawyers: On the theme of names matching jobs, Jeremy Allen of Standard Chartered Bank told us of a firm of solicitors in Leamington Spa, UK, called Wright Hassal and Co.

"Similarly, there is a long-established firm of English estate agents going by the name of Doolittle and Dally," he said.

Top Ole: Did you see in *Business Post* that the boss of Saga Furs is called Ole Borreson?

What do his friends say when they want to refer to him in an affectionate way? Ole Ole Borreson?

Really, Truly: Howard Wu of Asco Trade Typesetting, Quarry Bay was amused to get a business card from someone called Truly Man of Southport Industrial, a furniture company in Wan Chai.

One would imagine Truly Man to be a real macho piece of beefcake.

She isn't.

Ring in: While poring over the latest Hong Kong company results, we noticed that the chairman of Hop Hing Holdings is Hung Hap-hip.

What does he say when he picks up the phone? "Hi. Hung Hap-hip, Hop Hing?"

He could go into rap music.

Anyone for Terry?: Writer Simon Winchester and theatrical impresario Derek Nimmo were chatting at David Tang's house in Sai Kung. Mr Nimmo said one of his contacts had tried to phone a member of his party at the Hong Kong Hilton.

Caller: May I speak to Terry Scott?
First hotel voice: Wait a minute.
(Click. Whirr. Beep.)

Second hotel voice: Tennis Court.

Mind you, if you consider the fact that 'n', 'l' and 'r' are often interchangeable in oriental languages, the actor's name really could be Tenni Scourt.

Hello, hello: We came across a laundry in Old Bailey Street, Hong Kong, called "Wei Wei".

Imagine if it ever expanded enough to get a professional receptionist.

Wei Wei: Wei Wei. Wei?
Caller (confused): Wei?
Wei Wei (repeats): Wei Wei. Wei?
Caller (confused): Wei?
Etc.

Loose crew: Several readers have brought to our attention the fact that a name-badge-wearing crew member working in Delifrance at Queensway Plaza, Hong Kong, has been given the name "S. Crew Ying".

People are so cruel.

McSpaced-out: Philippa Robeson of Aberdare Consultants has been reading name-tags at McDonald's.

"If you go into the branch in North Point, you could be served by an Alien," she said.

The staff are pretty unusual, too.

Hole lotta trouble: A former Cathay Pacific Airways purser was reminiscing about a stewardess called Anis, and her colleague, who had dubbed herself Vibro.

You can image the reaction among passengers when their names were mentioned on the speakers.

"I made sure never to mention them both in one announcement," said the former purser.

Why not?: John Taylor of Robinson Road recently advertised for a secretary and was amused to get an application from the delightfully named "Bonkie Yu Wai-mee".

That's not a name. That's a conversation.

Poison pen: Dickson Hall of the Hong Kong office of the Government of British Columbia picked up his newspaper and scanned the front page. The main story warned about the dangers of chlorine in Hong Kong.

The next thing he picked up was a brochure sent out all over Hong Kong this week by a mobile phone salesperson at NEC. Her name: Chlorine Ho.

Can this be coincidence? "I wonder what effect she has on customers?" he asked. "She must be a gas."

Phil Rosenberg of Great Wall Graphics, who received the same brochure, suggested that Ms Ho add a little '2' between the letters of her surname.

Headlinewriterwallah: Noel Rands of Gallery 7, Glenealy, had a remarkable entry for our series of memorable names.

In India during the period of the British Raj, many workers were given names based on the product or service they offered.

Thus an umbrella seller would be called "Mr Brollywallah" (wallah means salesperson). These nicknames later became their actual names.

A sister of Noel's colleague, Janjri Trivedi, was at school with a girl whose name was (take a deep breath) Yasmin Sodabottlepopbottleopenerwallah.

Imagine if she ever came here and had to spell her name down the telephone to Hong Kong secretaries.

Misnomers: Yasmin Sodabottlepopbottle-etc may not be the weirdest name to emerge in this column.

We've just come across this list of certified real names, taken from an American population census taken in the year 1790.

Wanton Blount
Mourning Chestnut
Comfort Clock
Sermon Coffin
Boston Frog
Anguish Lemmon
Thomas Purity
Ruth Shaves
Thomas Simmers
Sarah Simpers
Truelove Sparks

That Sermon Coffin sounds a laugh-a-minute guy.

Meanwhile, Norman Brent of WH Consultants came across the name card of an employee of Fortress called More Kwok.

"I've been trying to puzzle out whether friend More is wishful or boastful," he said.

We imagine More's parents had a lot of children, and when another one popped out, exclaimed: "More?!"

A wash-out: Food writer Ken Barrett tells us that the new Domino's Pizza which has just opened in Glenealy, Central, has a young man named Mucky Ngan assembling the pizzas.

"Mercifully, he doesn't appear to live up to his name," said Ken.

No wonder they've got problems in Yugoslavia. Did you notice the name of the general who has just taken over as defence minister?

Zivota Panic.

You would have thought General Panic was exactly what they wanted to avoid.

A date with a date: Hong Kong economist Andrew Freris adds to our list of memorable names:

"The 1930s matinee idol Frederick March had a son named Frederick March III, (pronounced 'The Third', a common practice in the United States).

"At some stage, the son was romantically linked with the actress Tuesday Weld. Had they married, her name would have changed to 'Tuesday March The Third'."

Well, at least that's one date the husband should have had no trouble remembering.

McDoc: The reason why employees of McDonald's Hong Kong have the strangest names continues to elude us.

An efficient young manageress at the branch in Connaught Road, we noticed yesterday, is called "Doctor". If you collapse and someone asks: "Is there a doctor in the house?", prepare to be brought back to life by a lady wielding a chip pan.

He wears the trousers: Richard Needham, the personable new British Trade Commissioner in Hong Kong, has been entertaining local dignitaries.

He said that many of the present generation of decision-makers in the UK government were from business backgrounds.

"What business were you in?" one of his fellow diners asked.

"I sold knickers at Marks and Spencer," he replied, with perfect equanimity. "They used to call me 'Knickers Needham'."

What a frank gentleman.

If his middle name had been Ulysses, M & S could have used his name as an advertisement: "Knickers? U. Needham."

More name problems: the people of Thailand always get a good laugh out of President Arap Moi of Kenya, says Roy Stall of Hong Kong Polytechnic.

"His surname, unfortunately, translates as 'pubic hair'," he said.

"Come to think of it, President 'Bush' doesn't raise many giggles."

Soft 'n' sexy: Software engineer Dave Brown of QAD Asia-Pacific called a local software company in Hong Kong to be greeted by a female voice saying: "Hello sexy."

Dave was taken aback. While he was trying to think of a rejoinder, she continued: "This is sexy."

Anyway, Dave called and gave us the telephone number, and we called it too.

"This is sexy," she said.

We fully agreed that it was. But things were not what they seemed.

The receptionist was not expressing her feelings about making conversation on the phone. She was answering the way anyone would if they worked for a company called CXC Software Engineering.

Devilish: Paul Claughan of Stanley sent us the namecard of an employee of the Fortune Court chain of Chinese restaurants. Her name is Angel Sin.

"A fallen Angel? Or just another oxymoron?" asked Paul.

Firm warning: The latest Hongkong Government Gazette includes a warning about a company which is in danger of being struck off the register.

Its name: Moronicus Limited.

It would be a tragedy to lose a firm with such a great name. Would its directors kindly take whatever steps are needed.

Burst bubble: Keith Taylor of the Hong Kong branch of Generali was peering at the Government lists of companies going bust. He found that the Connaught Aerated Water Co had decided to go into liquidation.

"It is a sign that the froth has gone off the market," he opined.

Despair ING: NMB Bank has changed its name. It now wants to be called ING Bank.

This is an enormously bad idea for various reasons.

1. It is a pronounceable acronym, so instead of saying "I. N. G. Bank", people will say "Ing Bank".

2. The temptation for graffiti scribblers (and headline writers) to add a verb as a prefix will be irresistible.

3. Reader David Chappell points out that people may pronounce it the continental European way, in which case it will become "Bank ING".

4. "And what if a banking magazine gives it a four-star rating?" added David. "It will become ****ING Bank."

Writs cracker: Griff Griffith noticed in the Supreme Court Writs list that there is a certain Hong Kong company being sued over a dispute over "Goods Sold and Delivered".

The name of the company: Overbill Enterprises Ltd.

Frightful: Keith Maxted of Asco Group of Companies noticed a new enterprise open in Tsim Sha Tsui recently.

The firm is called Fairtrade. But according to the sign outside their office, they are employed as "Fright Consultants".

"I can only assume that the Fright Consultants offer a counselling service to the victims of Club Yobo," said Keith.

Club Yobo is the Korean Karaoke Club in the Crystal Centre, just a few yards away.

Swift byte: A new computer graphics company has been launched in Hong Kong called Wooden and Filling.

They would be great in the fast food business.

Another world: If you get the booklet of Christmas promotions from the Sheraton hotel, you may be shocked if you open it in the middle fold.

This page has the headline: "CELEBRATE AT SOMEPLACE ELSE"

No, they are not being unfriendly. It is the name of their pub.

Brotherly love: Don't be shocked by the sign on a shopfront in Wan Chai Road. It isn't really a "BROTHEL".

The "R" and the "Y" have fallen off the signboard belonging to a photography shop called "BROTHERLY"

Wow is me: We came across a firm called Wowful Air Conditioning of Kowloon (note they are Wowful, as opposed to Woeful).

There is also a trading firm called Wot Yu. Was this the result of a surprise meeting between the company manager and an official of the Companies Registry?

Official: "I'm here to ask you what you would like your

company called."
   Manager: "Wot? Yu?"

Number's up: We see that C. Itoh has changed its name. From now on it wants to be known as Itochu.
   The company's announcement gives no clues as to what it means, but one of our contacts says it is what a Japanese banker says when he sneezes.
   First Banker: Itochu!
   Second Banker (bowing): Gesundheit, banker-san.

Not you, them: We are much concerned about a listing plan for Hong Kong leather goods firm Gofuku.
   Brokers, we reckon will have genuine marketing problems with such an awkward name.
   Maiden aunt: What shall I invest in?
   Broker: Gofuku.
   Maiden Aunt: !

Cleans whiter: The campaign to clean up the words of rap music has spread to Hong Kong, reports tax consultant Fred Fredricks.
   Or at least that is what he assumes, since a shop has opened in the Admiralty Centre called Sing Clean.
   In the same shopping centre he found a shoe store called Payee.
   "I bet they get a lot of cheques made out to them," he said.

Ferry funny: Reader Stuart Savage was on Hong Kong's Star Ferry the other day, wondering how some of these aged vessels on the harbour stay afloat.
   Then a boat caught his eye.
   "The captain has obviously been reading Lai See's arti-

cles on catchy names, because he had named his boat the LEE KEE," said Stuart. "It looked it, too."

Another alien? A firm called Siera Electronics announced in Hong Kong yesterday that it had sold its trademarks. It is registered in Hong Kong as a proprietor of "philosophical instruments".

What is a philosophical instrument? Is Tom Lee now selling electric pianos that muse on their own existence?

Incidentally, the deed of assignment says the Siera trademarks have been sold to "Philips Gloeilampenfabrieken, a Naamlooze Vennootschap".

There are no clues as to what this means.

Isn't Naamlooze Vennootschap the name of a character in "Hitchhiker's Guide to the Galaxy"? If not, it should be.

EIE say, EIE say, EIE say: The Iyo Bank of Japan announced the opening of a Hong Kong office in Pacific Place. This lot are not far away from the finance boys of EIE.

If they got together they could run a joint venture called EIE-Iyo.

By coincidence, a high ranking member of the *corps diplomatique* told us yesterday that he had spotted a company on Kwun Tong Road called EI-EI-O. It would be good name for a chain of clinics which sell exotic medicines, such as powdered deer testicles.

Their slogan could be: "With a quack quack here and a quack quack there."

Not the officers' mess: When it comes to fine dining, we believe that it is the food that counts, not the decor.

Which is why we wholeheartedly approve of the new restaurant which has opened in Hennessy Road, Wan Chai: "The Healthy Mess."

Least expected use of an offensive term: Several readers have been curious about the emergence of a property firm in Hongkong called "Chinky".

Chinky advertises in our classified pages, and sends letters to property-owners signed "Chinky Property Consultants".

Curious people who phone Chinky's office in the Valley Centre, Morrison Hill Road, Wan Chai, are greeted by a bright voice saying: "Chin-ky!"

Is this some dreadfully racist *gweilo* muscling into the local flat-trading scene? No. Local businesswoman Liza To decided to form a property dealership, and went to a fortune teller in Sha Tin to get some mystical guidance on the name of her company.

The old sage gave her two Chinese characters which are pronounced Jun Kay.

The closest English transliteration, since she couldn't call it Junkie, was Chinky. Her overseas Chinese clients, who were fluent in American slang, were shocked by the name.

But Liza defended it, saying she is using the word without any disparaging intention, much like the word *gweilo* is used.

"And there is another meaning for 'Chinky' in English," she said.

"When a lot of coins get together, the sound they make is chink-chink. I thought that that made it sound like exactly the right name for a property agency."

Thick as a brick: Hilary Ford of Simpson Marine, a yachtbroking firm, was browsing through "Dun's Guide — Key Decision-Makers in Hong Kong Businesses 1992." This lists the address of the head office of Circle K as the "Witty Commercial Building" in Tung Choi Street, Mongkok.

"This building must be one up on the 'intelligent' buildings we keep reading about, if it has a sense of humour as well," said Hilary.

Cotton industry: Tax consultant Fred Fredricks of Wo On Lane tells us about an American couple in the garment trade who used to visit Hong Kong on business.

His family name was Cotton, and his mother had christened him King.

King Cotton was an ideal name for someone in the rag trade.

But even more remarkable was the fact that her first name was Polly, and her middle name Esther. Her married name? Polly Esther Cotton.

Fred, before coming to Hongkong, spent some time in Oklahoma, which he says is full of towns with unbelievable names. There's a town called Bug Tussle and another called Whiz Bang.

"On the road from Red Rock to Still Water, I used to pass a signpost which said: 'Lost Creek: one mile west'."

Fred also knew of a town in Wyoming called Crazy Woman — a name which got a lot of people in trouble.

Wyoming wife: Where ya' goin', John-boy?

Wyoming husband: Crazy Woman.

Wyoming wife: How dare ya' speak to me like that? (Thumps him.)

Mad Englishman: Our search for the most bizarrely named town in the world continues, with the UK taking a leading position.

There are all real places in Britain:

Yonder Bognie; Turton Bottoms; Chew Magna; Criddling Stubbs; Buttsash; Wool; and Fugglestone Saint Peter.

The last of these sounds like the sort of expletive an angel might use in an argument.

Saint Peter: Fie on you, Gabriel!

Gabriel: Fugglestone, Saint Peter!

No wonder Hongkong lawyer Tim Soutar was skulking around guiltily.

Those embarrassing names of English towns such as Idle, Pratts Bottom and the villages outside Hope (always referred to as "beyond Hope") — his family background includes ALL of them.

The peripatetic Soutar family appears to choose homes by the ludicrousness level of the place names.

Mr Soutar, who works in Central, said: "I hope the fact that my background includes a place beyond Hope, and homes in Idle and Pratts Bottom, does not mean that I am now a disillusioned Idle Pratt."

Whoops: Canadian Paul Paskewitz of Mutualpress, Wellington Street, tells us that there is a town in Quebec called St Louis de Ha Ha.

It sounds as if the founding fathers of Quebec were solemnly naming their towns when one of them suddenly let loose a guffaw.

That wonderful jazz composer George Shearing (he wrote "Lullaby of Birdland") was in Hongkong recently, staying at the Regent.

The hotel's PR manager Sheila Arora tells us that Mr Shearing has the same fascination for odd English place names as Lai See.

Mr Shearing gave her the following poem, which is a homesick Englishman's version of the Lord's Prayer.

How far is

The White Hart from Hendon?
Harrow Road be thy name.
Thy Kingston come;
Thy Wimbledon;
In Erith as it is in Devon.
Give us this day our Maidenhead
And forgive us our Westminsters,
And lead us not into Thames Ditton,
But deliver us from Yeovil.
For thine is the Kingston,
The Purley and the Crawley
For Ivor and Ivor,
Crouch End.

Hot spot: Terry Crossman of *Asian Career Journal* tells us that there is a town in Michigan called Hell.

Everyone who comes from there sounds like the title of a cheap horror movie: The Women's Institute from Hell, the Priest from hell, the School Bus from hell, etc.

Mad dogs and . . . : Surely the ultimate listing of unbelieveable-but-true English place names, comes from Simon Thompson, director of Hong Kong-based Passim Design Ltd, which follows:

Utterly English:
Upton Snodsbury; Wilkin Throod; Puttocks End; Snape Watering; Hazelbury Plucknett; Swaffham Bulbeck; Grafty Green; Gussage All Saints; Quadring Eaudike and Steeple Bumstead.

Horribly Embarrassing for those who live there:
Hogspit Bottom; Knackers Hole; Tit Hill; Puddle Town; Cock and End; The Throat; Misery Corner; Bog Town; Lit-

tle Comfort; Droop; Wyre Piddle and Pig Oak.

Just Plain Daft:
Plucks Gutter; Trunch; Nether Wallop; Gweek; Great Snoring; Little Snoring; Bleet; Over Wallop; Finkle; Knook; Piffs Elm and The Mumbles.

Thought-Provoking:
Simons Bath; Roast Green; Coed Eva; Chew Magna; Marsh Gibbon; Hole-in-the-Wall; Grub Street; Brassknocker; Cackle Street; Blackboys; Dial Post; Pease Pottage; Inkpen; Clapworthy; Come-to-Good and Custards.
There's even a UK town called Eau Well.

Fun towns: David Hager of Stanley used to live in Minnesota, in the United States.
"There are two towns there called Fertile and Climax," he said. "Some years ago, after an auto collision, the local paper called the unfortunate headline: Fertile Woman Dies in Climax."
The moral majority were not amused.

Shapely pair: In Illinois there are towns called Normal and Oblong. Which is why a headline from a local paper in that area once carried the headline: Normal Man Married Oblong Woman.

Lovers' lanes: "I'll tell you something even most New Yorkers don't know," said Richard Rund, boss of FOB Products in Kowloon.
"At the northern tip of New York, just above Washington Heights, there is an area called Inwood.
"It has two streets which intersect: Cumming Street and Seaman Avenue."

Shop soiled: Carey Leonard of standard Chartered Bank tells us of a village in Shropshire, England, called Knockin.

"This little place has only one shop," he said.

You can probably guess its name.

Hills are alive: Norman Wingrove of Kowloon Bay tells us there's a town called Soldier's Bottom in Hampshire, UK. Sounds like an unpleasant place.

Keith Wills of HMS, Wan Chai, said: "Don't forget Pity Me and Shiny Row in Tyne and Wear, Seldom Seen in Cumbria, and the sinister Unthank, also in Cumbria."

He said that there were three mountains in what used to be Cumberland, called: Cockup, Little Cockup and Great Cockup.

There are several expats in the Hong Kong administration whom we suspect come from these mystic hills.

LORD OF ALL HE SURVEYS

If I ever have to get a REAL job instead of abusing this typewriter, I know exactly what it is going to be. I am going to be a Market Researcher. This is the new cutting-edge job of the 1990s.

Those slinking-around jobs which USED to be thought glamorous, such as private eye, insider trader, Finance Minister of Japan and so on, have lost their allure.

No. Today's most talked-about topics on the street are the amazing-but-true factoids dug up by the collectors of "consumer intelligence", those shadowy, behind-the-scenes dealers in the bizarre ephemera of real life.

Ever since I became interested in this, I have been making a close study of pre-digested factoids, and have been fascinated by the implicit operations that must have been performed to collect them.

Here are some examples culled recently from newspapers.

1. The average woman kisses 79 men before she marries one.

Now assuming that most married women start dating in their mid-teens and get married in their mid- to late- twenties, our hard-working Market Researcher had a period of about 12 to 15 years in which all kisses, however perfunctory, had to be recorded. We are talking about a difficult and ambitious survey here. I would find it impossible to believe that the researcher was actually present with his digital data recorder at each of these occurrences. He may have just taken the word of the woman being kissed. Or he may have worked it out by interviewing EXTREMELY large numbers of men, and discovering that each woman appeared on the lists of 79 men.

2. The average man grows 25 feet of hair in his lifetime.

A man's hair grows at different speeds throughout his life, so the Market Researcher could not have measured growth for a couple of hours and then extrapolated the figures. Did he pay someone a fee to NOT have his hair cut for his lifetime, say 75 years? If so, there is must a fascinating story to be told about what the chap did with his 25 feet of hair. Did he wear it in rings around his midriff? Alternatively, the Market Researcher could have made an arrangement with barbers, so that the hair of the selected representative Average Man was collected every time it was cut through his lifetime.

3. The average person, including each member of the Royal family, expels 500 ml of internal air every day.

The bit that intrigued me about this one was the bit about the Royal family. As far as I know, you are not entitled to speak to a member of the Royal family until he or she has spoken to you. So our courageous Market Researcher must have had to hang around in the environs of Buckingham Palace, possibly for days, until the Queen said: "Arise, thou loyal subject," or whatever she uses to open conversations with. But how would he have put his question in a delicate enough manner as to not risk offending her? "Excuse me, Ma'am, but I am a Market Researcher and I wish to know if Your Highness has burped today, or expelled gaseous substances in any other way, and also approximate details of the volume please." I believe treason is still a crime punishable by death in England.

4. The average woman now uses 21 cosmetic and hygiene products in her daily morning routine.

Now this is a good old-fashioned piece of consumer information, usable by manufacturers, retailers and investors. The Market Researcher, I imagine, would have picked it up by hiding behind the shower curtain in several hundred households, and simply counting the items used. This is presumably a low-level job, given to apprentices in the trade.

5. The average US$50 banknote now has traces of cocaine on it, since the habit of sniffing drugs through rolled-up notes has become common among well-heeled drug-users.

How did they come across this fact? Did a Market Researcher notice that bank-tellers counting the money were getting high? Does the Federal Reserve employ an olefaction inspector to sniff the money, in case it smells unsavoury?

6. The average passionate kiss uses 12 calories.

Calories are measured by burning an item of food and measuring the amount of energy given off. Clearly, one cannot burn the participants in the above factoid. Is it a matter of weighing the couple in their pre-kiss state, allowing their lips to press heavily together for a minute, and then weighing them again? Can a weighing machine detect such a minute change? Or was it done by having a "control" group of people only receiving diet food, while another group receives the same food but also gets kissed by the waiting staff?

This last example must give rise to a subsidiary question: how does one volunteer to be take part in market research? I am extremely average, but have never been approached. There must be more positive action I can take than just standing around in shopping malls trying to look like a voracious consumer.

What sort of people get chosen? There must be a firm out there, called something like Amazing Factoids Market Research Inc, who can answer this question for me.

WHAT EVERY TRAVELLER IN ASIA SHOULD KNOW

A tip on getting by in Bali from Hal Archer of the Hong Kong Channel. What do you do if someone comes up to you and says: "Have you had a bath?"

Clamp your armpits to your sides?

No. He or she may be using a traditional late afternoon greeting in Balinese which actually means "Hi".

Or, it may mean what you first thought.

Worst contribution to the America First campaign: Photojournalist David Chappell flew into Hong Kong from California.

In the toilet of his Delta Airlines flight was the sign: "Do Not Throw Foreign Articles into the Flushing Toilet."

(US-made objects apparently zip down into the sewage tank without any trouble.)

Thai breaker: Travellers heading to Thailand should consult a Thai phrase book owned by Ted and Karen Eliot of Stanley, Hong Kong. Vital sentences you need to get by in Thailand include:

Is this a bivouac?
Bandage my wound.
Hide my parachute.
Tell him nothing but that important friends have to see him.
If we cannot trust a man,
(a) wink your right eye
(b) place your left hand on your stomach.

Karen's favourite is an all-purpose sentence designed to help you make friends in a war, whoever is winning.

We are here to help them in the struggle, on the side of:
(a) the free world.
(b) the United States.
(c) the allies.
(d) Freedom.
(e) God.

The most baffling phrase in the book:

When does snow usually start falling? Are the avalanches dangerous?

Avalanches aren't common in tropical Thailand.

Rice paper: There was a story on the Reuters news-wire about the boom in rice-growing in Vietnam. The source was an official publication called "The *Sunday Vietnam News*, published on Monday", the report says.

One cannot help but wonder why they don't call it the *Monday Vietnam News*.

Most provocative etymological discovery: Came across *Llama Life*, a journal devoted to llamas, which it describes as a woolly-haired, docile, happy-faced creature found on undulating terrain.

Surely the word llama must be derived from Lamma island in Hong Kong, also associated with woolly-haired, docile, happy-faced creatures found on undulating terrain?

Dangerous roads: If you ask a business person for advice as to where to set up an office in Vietnam, you may think you hear them reply: "Go to that damn street in Ho Chi Minh City."

What they are actually doing is advising you to go to one of the business areas, a road in District One called Ton That Dam Street.

Or, he may have meant what you thought he said.

Worst geographers: This we found hard to believe, except it happened to us. The National Geographic Society, the world's most famous explorers, held a grand dinner at the Mandarin Oriental hotel in Hong Kong.

Guests of honour included some of the most senior editors from that august publication, arguably the world's foremost authority on geographic matters.

And guess what address they printed on the invitation we received?

Mandarin Oriental Hotel
5, Connaught Road
Hong Kong, China.

Hymnalong-with-Jesus: Popped into one of Jakarta's main Roman Catholic churches, the Geredja Canisius, on Christmas Day.

There were no carol books and not a hymn book to be seen anywhere.

When the service started, lyrics appeared on the wall above the priests, with the help of an overhead projector.

The congregation sang along, karaoke-style, led by priests crooning into microphones on a raised stage.

Instead of hymns or carols, the songs were modern guitar-backed numbers, such as that Johnny Mathis chart-topper *When a Child is Born.*

Before the Christmas Day mass ended, the priest instructed the congregation to "give a big hand" to the sound system people.

Yes, karaoke is taking over the world, and, very probably, the world after.

Frying high: Charlotte Woolley of South Island School lunched at Saigon Airport, where the menu offered:

Sauteed Uterus With Mushrooms.

Screw Duck.

The restaurant doesn't bother with fussy terms such as "rare". The next item was:

Underdone Liver.

Lada them than us: Investors in Taiwan have set up a company to introduce motorists to a new driving sensation — the Lada. The much joked-about car, to be imported by Taiwan Lada Automobile Industry Co, will be a first taste of Russian motoring for Taiwanese drivers.

Taiwan has not yet discovered Lada jokes or Skoda jokes. Visitors to Taiwan should kindly refrain from telling such jokes until the new firm has found its feet.

Worst sweat shop: Nissen Davis, Hong Kong executive with McDonnell Douglas, was reading a tourist brochure for Sichuan province, which said the province was "endowed with mild climate and adequate perspiration".

Has the Hong Kong Water Supplies Dept considered this source of moisture?

"Drought holds little terror for the farmers of Sichuan province," said Mr Davis.

Well, it gives a new meaning to the phrase "by the sweat of one's brow".

Vital phrases for visitors to Indonesia: These are provided by Paul Aldrich of Chase Manhattan Bank in Hong Kong, from *How to Master the Indonesian Language* by A.M. Almatsier:

Stapa yang memasang TV jika kamu tidak ada di rumah?
Who turns on the TV when you are not at home?
Hurra! Lampu sudah hidup.
Hurrah! The light is on.
Anjing hitam saya sudah mati.
My black dog is dead already.

You'll find yourselves using these phrases again and again.

Manila envelope: We were having a debate the other day on the alternative spellings used by our friends from Manila.

The country is spelt Philippines, the people are Filipinos, the females are Filipinas and a commonly used general adjectival form is Philippine.

Unconnected to this, a shipping company in Singapore just happened to send us some material by Federal Express. It was marked with our address in Hong Kong and the shipping firm's name, Offshore Pipelines.

It failed to arrive and came to light some days later in the Philippines.

The unmistakable implication is that someone at Federal Express decided that Pipelines was yet another alternative spelling of that country's name, pronounced "Pip-e-lin-es".

For all we know, it probably is.

Herman's hermit: Freelance writer Neal McGrath of Sai Ying Pun picked up a wonderful English study book in Malaysia called *Daily Conversation and Words*.

This gives the Malaysian student snatches of realistic conversation in an idiomatic way, so that he or she can blend in completely unnoticed, like a native English speaker.

When visiting a friend:
A: Excuse me, sir, is the owner's at home?
B: I don't know, please peep through the key's hole.
A: No lights. It was very dark. I am sure no one at home.
Casual conversation:
A: What are you doing, Herman?
B: I not doing nothing.
A: Are you thinking about anything?
B: No, I'm not.
How to meet girls:
A: Shall we go for a walk?
B: All right, that is a good idea. Who are we going with?
A: Our sweethearts.
B: I don't agree.
A: Why?
B: Their parent won't allow them.
A: It is impossible.
B: Are you sure?
A: Yes, indeed.
In the workplace:
A: Sir, there is a calling for you.
B: Where that calling from?

Don't know about you, but we have such conversations almost daily.

Spit roasted: Marc Rouen of *Business Traveller* has been collecting menu items from around the region. Here are his

favourites:
APPETISERS:
Half Fresh Grapefruit;
Shrimps in Spit.
MAIN COURSES:
Dreaded Veal Cutlet;
Bacon and germs;
English Teak and Kidney Pie;
Potatos in Shirt.
DESSERTS:
Tarts of the House;
Sweat from the Trolley.

Have a smoke, son, we want to show we care: If a Shanghai Airlines aircraft is late, the top man in the firm will drive to Shanghai airport and personally express his sorrow to passengers, an official told us.

"General manager Mr He will go to the airport and apologise to the customers himself," vowed Raymond Zhou, assistant to company boss He Pengnian.

The level of service to passengers had improved markedly, delegates to the Asian Air Finance Conference at Hong Kong's Hotel Furama agreed.

"I remember a trip on Yugoslav Airlines 10 years ago lasting three hours," said one attendee. "The only sustenance provided was an ancient bar of chocolate and some strange peanuts. These came in an attack-proof foil bag that appeared to be a spin-off from some weapons research. On touchdown, not one packet had been prised open."

Eric Stone, deputy editor of *Asian Business*, said: "I flew on a domestic airline from South Kalimantan a few years ago. The meal was a bowl of rice with some peanut sauce, plus a packet of clove cigarettes.

"Every passenger got a packet of cigarettes, including the

six-year-old boy next to me."

These days you would probably get the company president in the aisle, lighting the kid's cigarette.

Down Under the breadline: Much of what we read from Australia just recently concerns that country's prospects of divorcing itself from the British monarchy and becoming a republic.

After looking at the state of the Australian economy, one thing puzzles us.

They seem to have left out the word "banana".

Fuzzy outlook: What are we to make of this? There is a special one-day seminar booked on November 4, 1992 at the Hong Kong Productivity Council office in Tat Chee Avenue, Kowloon.

The speaker is Professor Kaoru Hirota.

He is director of the Japanese Fuzzy Society.

Anybody know what this is?

Are the members fuzzy in the sense of having short, springy hair, or in the sense of invoking warm and wholesome feelings?

We feel we qualify in both departments, so would like to start a Hong Kong Fuzzy Society.

Other potential members: film buff Paul Fonoroff; Hong Kong Bank spokesman Bob Sherbin; United Democrat Lee Wing-tat; and finance writer Gareth Hewett.

Load of yahng poo: Mary Hoppin of the ASM Group, Hong Kong, has just got hold of a book called *Chinese Without a Teacher*, published in 1939.

These were considered vital phrases in those days:
Is there any opium? *Yo yahng-yo mayo?*
There are 200 bales of grey shirtings. *Yo ur pi p'ee yahng*

poo.
>   This cart is dirty. *Chayka ch'awahzah.*
>   Your animals are bad. *Neety shungk'o poo how.*
>   I want to have chow-chow now. *Shendzi you ch'irp fahn.*
>   Roast two pheasants. *K'ow layanga yay-chee.*
>   This cook is not a good one. *Chayka ch;oodza poo-how.*
>   The coolie is also very lazy. *K'oolee yay hun lahntaw.*

We would copy out some more of this hilarious book, but we have just looked at the clock and we want to have chow-chow now.

Foreign parts: Editor Linda Pelham of Wordpower was standing in a long queue at the headquarters of Hong Kong Bank.

Suddenly her eagle eye caught the electronic message board which was reeling off information.

It said: "To avoid long queues during lunch hours, month ends and periods near pubic holidays, may we suggest banking with us during mornings instead?"

What are pubic holidays, anyway? Do they mean trips to Bangkok?

Material world: Adrian McCarron of Original Vision, Wellington Street, was looking for orchids from Vietnam in *Vietnam Trade Directory 1992* when he came across a firm in Hanoi.

This has the remarkably honest name: "Hanoi Material Exploitation Co."

It lists its main products as: "Materials and Substandard Materials."

A huge number of Hong Kong firms do exactly the same lines of business.

If only our people could be this up-front.

Most Shocking Revelation to Asian Yuppies: The debate about the pronunciation of Polo by Ralph Lauren was finally settled in 1991. Was it Ralph La-WREN? Or Ralph LORen?

Neither. His name was revealed to be Ralph Lifshitz.

Least attractively titled show: In the Bali Beach Hotel on December 30, 1991, we spotted some Hong Kong people turning up their noses at an activity called a "Joged Bum Bung" scheduled to be demonstrated at a hotel.

This, in fact, is a cultural show, although who can blame them for feeling uptight in these days of audience participation?

Heavy petting: It's the new sensation in Indonesian tourism: The Copulated Elephant. Dr Judith Mackay of Sai Kung tells us of a holiday show by that name in Way Kambas, in the province of Lampung.

Love-making elephants are "the Superstar tourism object in Way Kambas" according to a brochure from the Tourism Department of Lampung.

Spectators are taken to a tower, from which they look down on to a bull-elephant and a she-elephant being friendly.

Dr Mackay has read about the Copulated Elephant but has not witnessed it.

The brochure enthuses: "This is the first erotical scene that is available in the world and be included in the tourist industry programme."

The male elephant's contribution is two-thirds the length of his trunk, and revolves freely, rather like a carpenter's awl.

Talking of beastly acts, the first shipment of Larry Feign's cartoon book *How the Animals Do It*, which also features elephants, quickly sold out in Hong Kong.

All this interest must be proof that Asians have a healthy interest in romantic matters. Sort of.

Best-laid plan: Patrick Waterfield, Hong Kong-based executive for Guerlain, was in Tokyo and had to get to Narita Airport in a hurry, to catch a flight back to the territory. Heavy snow was falling and clogging up the transport system.

He took a taxi to the airport bus depot at Hakozaki. Then he left the taxi waiting, its meter running, while he dashed in to the bus ticket desk.

"Is the departure of the bus delayed because of the snow? My flight, CX505 leaves at 5.35 pm to Hong Kong," he asked.

"No delay," said the girl at the counter.

He dashed back to the taxi and paid it off. As it disappeared, he picked up his luggage and headed off to get the bus to the airport.

The counter girl told him he couldn't.

"But you told me there were no delays," he said.

"There are no delays," she replied. "But the buses are full."

Heave ho: Got a copy of *Bangladesh News* from the Hong Kong office of that nation.

"Prime Minister Begum Khaleda Zia has heaved lavish praise on the garments industries," it says.

Do they mean "heaped"? Or is Mr Zia following the example of President George Bush on his recent trade tour of Japan?

Uproarious: Travellers reaching Shanghai are handed instructions from the Shanghai Public Security Bureau.

"No guest is allowed to up anyone for the night, or let anyone use his/her own bed in the hotel," it says.

If you can't sleep in your own bed, whose bed do you sleep in?

Why're you staring? I'm only famous in Britain: The price of fame in Asia can be mere pocket money. This we heard from visiting UK disc jockey Simon Bates, who interviewed Lai See on his BFBS show recently.

Mr Bates noticed that people in Hong Kong and other places in Asia had taken to pointing at him in public places. But how on earth could they know who he was?

On a visit to Bombay, he eventually asked some gawkers in a restaurant why they were staring at him. "You're the video man," they said.

It all clicked into place. Simon had made some pocket money four years ago by presenting an announcement for the video-tape industry. It said children should not see adult films and so on, and was attached to the beginning of pre-recorded videos.

Large numbers of these were copied — often illegally — and spread all over Asia, including Hong Kong.

All of a sudden everyone knew his face.

Disc jockeys faced the challenge of interacting with the public just like journalists, Simon said.

On Christmas Day a doctor — a cancer specialist — contacted his studio and asked for some requests to be played for his patients. The engineer mislaid the names, and the message never made it on to the airwaves.

The furious doctor contacted the director-general of the BBC and complained.

Simon phoned him back. "I'm terribly sorry," he said. "It's just one of those things. If you give me the names again, I'll do them as soon as I can."

"You can't," spat the doctor. "They're all dead."

It was the only occasion in his life when Simon Bates was speechless.

Throwaway line: At the Splendid China show in Shenzhen, they know how to deal with litter louts, says reader Bill Lake, who recently returned from there.

"No littering in scenic spot area," it says. (It's okay to do it in the rest of Shenzhen.)

"Whoever violates rules will be subject to the proper disposal."

This must be a case of making the punishment fit the crime.

England, U.S.: Got a letter from the Centre for Migration Studies in Staten Island, New York.

It was addressed to "Hong Kong, the Federal Republic of China".

How about that. Even FULL-TIME experts in geographical movement don't know where we are.

Wish you were here - and we were there: Sai Kung photographer Chris Davis was reading a remarkable holiday brochure recently.

"People who like to take a holiday with a difference might be interested in the *1992 Explorer Magazine,* published by Travel Advice Ltd," he said.

This is a firm in Swire House which specialises in holidays for small groups.

A quote from the brochure: "Visit Historic Sarajevo.

"We bus into the picturesque town of Sarajevo, a medley of Muslim, Croats, Catholics and Orthodox Serbs. The old Turkish quarter captures our imagination: partly girded by a thick wall, its charm is its rambling disorganisation. White plaster houses, shuttered windows and slender minarets add the spice of Oriental traditional to a chaotic cluster of streets.

"Few places in Europe provide such diversity of landscapes and peoples in so small an area."

Chris reckons it must be one of those "adventure holidays".

Well, if you think rambling disorganisation is charming, Sarajevo has even more to offer these days.

Malt schmalt: Charlotte Woolley of South Island School went to Sulawesi (formerly Celebes) in darkest Indonesia for Lunar New Year.

In a shop in Ujang Pandang, she picked up a bottle of what purported to be Dutch whisky, the brand name of which was Mansion House Whisky.

The ingredients, in order, were:

1. *Water.*
2. *Ethyl Alcohol.*
3. *Whisky Concentrate.*
4. *Artificial Flavouring.*

So that's how you make whisky. You stir a bit of flavouring and instant whisky powder into some water.

So much for all those fussy secret Scottish recipes for maturing single malts for years in barrels.

Even more original was the room-service menu at the Sanno Airport Hotel in Jakarta. This listed, for lunch and dinner:

Soup
Special Delight
Sandwiches
Mouth Washed Compulsory
Fresh Fruit.

Charlotte reluctantly declined this. Special **Delight**

sounded fun, but she did not fancy the compulsory mouthwash.

What would they have done, sent up six burly guys to hold her down while another brushed her teeth?

Eggs rated: A local foodie tells us he was in Bangkok recently when he came across a restaurant offering "Joke With One Fresh Egg".

Being in need of a good laugh, he sat down and ordered it.

What arrived was a bowl of what Hong Kong people know as *juk,* or congee, with a raw egg in it.

"After tasting it, I realised that in culinary terms, the title was completely accurate," he said.

Service fault: There was a "Dear Guest" letter in the rooms of Phuket's largest resort, the Phuket Island Resort.

"Tennis knockers are available on request," it said.

What does this mean? Isn't this some sort of sporting injury which women get?

Follow the herd: Have you seen the travel firm which is operating out of Tung Ming Building, Des Voeux Road? It is called Bullocks Travel Ltd.

Sounds rather old fashioned, although it is still a popular method of travel in Calcutta, we believe.

Nip on to Nippon: Is the continual bleating from Beijing making you nervous? Move to Japan. That country's zany culture means there are lots of out-of-the-ordinary jobs available.

Karen Regelman, Tokyo-based *Variety* columnist, was looking through the job vacancy lists in newspapers there. She gave us a run-down of the top 10 wacky jobs commercially advertised at the moment.

1. Drug Tester. They pump you up. You get high and tell them what happens.

2. Professional Queuer. Yes, you *can* get paid for just hanging out.

3. Driver Taking Drunken Men Home. Keep obnoxiousness off the roads by putting it in your car.

4. Watcher of Advertising Balloons. Enjoy staring into the middle distance? One person is allowed to take up to three balloon-watching jobs simultaneously.

5. Nasty Phone Caller. People with grudges don't want their voices recognised — that's where you come in. You can earn the yen equivalent of $64 for each call.

6. Chimney Cleaner for a Crematorium. Careful when you are scraping off that sooty gunk. It may be a relative.

7. Sexual Guinea Pig. Get paid for what some people do for nothing under an alternative designation: marriage partner.

8. Sperm Donor. Men, you can get the equivalent of HK$6,500 per donation. University students are paid extra, since their sperm is assumed to be more intelligent.

9. Auxiliary Riot Police. You get real uniforms, but fake guns, and stand at the back.

10. Comfort Stylist. Pass your days in happy contemplation of toilets. Toilet design is considered an important job, since 30 per cent of Japanese toilets now shower, warm, and blow-dry your bottom.

Chosen race: Jenny Crisp of Island School heard this from a Qantas stewardess friend in Hong Kong:

A flight was in progress when the flight attendant noticed a disturbance in economy class.

She found that a deeply racist South African had found himself seated next to a black woman and her child.

The horrified man demanded the stewardess find him

another seat. He complained that his "blick" neighbours smelled bad.

The stewardess told him that all the other seats in economy were full.

At this news, the furious racist demanded she check business class, and the poor black woman burst into tears.

"I'll go and see, sir," said the stewardess.

She came back with a smile. "I've found some space in business class," she said.

He grinned and started to unbuckle his seat-belt.

"Please follow me, madam," she said to the black woman and her child, and upgraded them.

Up a gum tree: The careful people who run Singapore have finally realised that their ban on chewing gum may hit their cargo-handling trade. There's a risk that arch-rival Hong Kong may steal a march in the cut-throat world of international gum pushing.

So Singapore has amended its rules. You can now take chewing gum into Singapore, but only if you take it out again unchewed. You must put aside a pledge of S$10,000 while the elicit substance is in the country.

The gum must be kept locked up in a warehouse in a free-trade zone.

It can only be taken from one zone to another in completely covered, sealed vehicles. If you are taking the gum through Singapore into Malaysia, it must be escorted between the free-trade zone and the customs checkpoint.

Citizens with the popular Singapore surname Chew must be living in fear.

Duty free: India has knocked down a tariff barrier with China. Yak tails can now be freely traded at newly opened posts on the Sino-Indian border.

Beijing and New Delhi have been working to liberalise border trade between their countries.

Okay, so they haven't achieved as much as GATT, but it's a start.

Costliest freebie: There we were, sitting on the Far East Jetfoils boat to Macau, swiftly overtaking a fishing boat openly bobbing along with a Mercedes-Benz (not a joke).

"*Bo ji, bo ji,*" said the chap selling newspapers.

"*Ga fe, ga fe,*" said the chap selling coffee.

We ordered both. The newspaper man was terribly helpful, rushing downstairs to find a *South China Morning Post* for us, and the coffee seller was also eager to be of service.

And so they should be at the outrageous prices they were charging.

Or was this anything to do with the fact that we later noticed that the coffee machine was marked "Free" and the newspapers were all stamped with the word "Complimentary"?

Most unwellcoming offer: There was a mouthwatering supply of red persimmons on the fruit and vegetable stand at the Wellcome supermarket in Caine Road, Hong Kong.

But stuck in front of them was a sign which said "Permission: HK$5.90".

How ridiculous to expect shoppers to ask for permission – and pay a fee – before eating a piece of fruit.

We urge shoppers to flout this pointless rule.

Newer than new: Eva Tsang of the Hong Kong Trade Department's public relations office bought a shrimp salad sandwich from the Mandarin Oriental hotel on May 21, 1992.

The label said:

Packed on 22. 05.92.
That's what we call fresh in both senses of the word.

For the pot: News reaches us of a corporate party held recently in Beijing. Northwest Airlines celebrated a new air route which takes passengers from Beijing to the west coast of the United States.

Guest of honour was a senior official from the mayor's office in Beijing.

The American visitors gave a live American beaver to the guest to mark the occasion. This animal, unfortunately, could not attend, since it was still in quarantine.

Beijing insiders could be seen chuckling away. Why?

The chief guest's brother-in-law runs a restaurant in the city called Wild Animals. On the menu: exotic wildlife, cooked to your satisfaction.

Sea-view flat, 2br, 1 bath, a-c, sailing shortly: Illegal immigrants now come ready-packaged. "Signed, sealed, delivered, I'm yours," as the Stevie Wonder song goes.

Hong Kong seaport officials have been plagued by chaps who spring out of 40-foot long cargo containers and start running. And now the idea is being pinched by east Europeans heading for the West.

John Meredith, boss of Hong Kong International Terminals recalls three spectacular jack-in-the-box cases in Hong Kong, where illegal immigrants from China were found in "empty" transshipment boxes in Kwai Chung.

"They always end up with our security people chasing them around the terminal premises," he said.

All were caught.

There was a recent case in Antwerp in which a container was seen to have air-holes cut into it. The manifesto (cargo list) said it was a shipment of beer. Inside were six Romanians, who had whiled away the time getting the cargo inside them.

A container of stowaways found in Germany turned out to be pleasantly equipped for a long journey, complete with toilet facilities.

Interior designers from Hong Kong and Japan, used to making fittings for small spaces, would surely find a container (average length 40 feet) an easy challenge.

You'd probably get a choice of bedrooms.

Most unusual extra: Bank consultant Anne Wilkins received a brochure from computer distribution firm Microware USA Ltd of Quarry Bay, saying:

A thorough testing will be carried before delivering to our customers in order to provide Defects FREE on all Compaq products we sold.

Anne was impressed. "It is a good job they provide defects free, because I don't think anyone would pay for them."

Wales blubber: While Robert Chua's "Dianagate" tape was running on a pay-as-you-listen tape in Hong Kong, the entrepreneur was busy getting an actor and actress to work on a Cantonese version.

But how do you translate the Princess' nickname, "Squidgy", into Cantonese?

Having thought long and hard about this important question of world affairs, we would like to suggest *Sup Lum Pe Pe* ("wet and soft") or *Waat San San* ("texture of mucus").

We like to do our bit for the Royal family.

Wales-blubber II: The new Cantonese translation of the "Dianagate" scandal tape stumbled just where we said it would – on the Princess's nickname "Squidgy".

After much debate, the translators decided to add the English word to the Cantonese language.

But this was only after Matthew Marsh of Robert Chua Productions intervened.

He had popped into check how the translating was going, and found that "Squidgy" had been translated as if it had something to do with a certain multi-tentacled item of seafood.

Emicate yourself: Alan Chalkley, a financial writer based in Seymour Road, received a letter from Ravi Bushan of Rifacimento International.

This is a Delhi-based company putting together a book called *Reference Asia: Asia's Who's Who of Men and Women of Achievement.*

Mr Bushan writes: *"Reference Asia* in a number of volumes concatenated at intervals is aimed to congregate and emicate Asian fame and notability of its living people to emmove commendal and international understanding."

He wants US$61 per person to concatenate, emicate and emmove commensal understanding.

Achieving understanding does not appear to be something Mr Bushan is good at.

Shoe-be-doo-be-doo: Caddie Greiner was in The Landmark shopping centre in Hong Kong when she paused outside the Edinburgh shoe boutique and caught sight of a "Bride of Frankenstein" hair-do.

This could only mean one thing: Imelda Marcos was shopping in there.

"I couldn't resist the temptation and went inside for some female bonding," she said. "I couldn't find anything I liked."

This seemed to gel with Lai See's wife's maxim: "If the shoe fits, it's ugly."

But Big Imelda managed to quickly snap up three pairs of shoes for HK$3,600. She was later reported to have spent HK$45,000 on six pairs.

Incidentally, we hear that Mrs Marcos felt in need of a massage, but the masseurs on duty at the Hotel Conrad were all male.

It was decided that it would be improper for a man to knead the sacred flesh. The nearby Marriott hotel had to despatch a female masseuse to do the job.

Surely it is her accountant who needs the massage?

Snake in the grass causes a right pickle: Most people bring T-shirts home as souvenirs from trips. Not our friend Paul.

After a trip to Ho Chi Minh City, he decided to bring a deadly Vietnamese cobra back to Hongkong.

The thing had long been dead, but was perfectly preserved in a large jar of chemicals.

The Vietnamese use snakes as an aphrodisiac, but Paul insists this was not why he wanted it.

So there he was at the airport with the jar, carefully sealed and placed in a polythene bag, on the floor.

Suddenly, a blundering fool with a trolley comes by and rams the jar, which shatters.

The cobra, still soft and pliable, unwound itself slinkily on to the floor of the airport, looking very much alive.

Paul drew a veil over the scenes of mass pandemonium which followed at the airport.

Shortly afterwards, a colleague from the same firm, a chap called Evelyn, was scheduled to go to Vietnam. "Buy me a snake," said Paul, whose full identity we promised not to reveal.

Evelyn bought a new cobra in Ho Chi Minh City, and

took extra-special care negotiating his way through the airport. He carried it on to the plane and safely stowed it in the overhead locker.

Along came a Taiwanese businessman with heavy, hard briefcase, which he threw into locker.

Crash. Tinkle. Splash. Slither.

The ex-cobra uncoiled, hurtled out of the overhead locker and plonked itself across the laps of several passengers — once again giving an excellent impersonation of a healthy killer serpent in a playful mood.

Our informant again drew a veil over the ensuing scenes of terror, panicky evacuation and the lengthy postponement of the flight.

(Sounds like the normal ingredients of a Vietnamese Airlines trip to us.)

The inn crowd: Ken Atkinson of PCS International of Queen's Road, Hong Kong, was trying to book a hotel room in Hanoi.

Ken: Hello. I would like to reserve a room.

Hotel: Sorry. Our hotel is full.

Ken: But I haven't said when I wanted a room!

Hotel: Sorry. Goodbye.

Then there was a click as the hotel staffer hung up. Ken, amazed at this treatment, phoned again.

Ken: Hello — please don't hang up. I would like to reserve a room from March 1st.

Hotel: Sorry. Our hotel is full today.

Ken: But I DON'T WANT a room today. I want one next Monday.

Hotel: Sorry. We are full today.

Ken: No, not today, next Monday.

Hotel: Oh. You booked a room next Monday?

Ken: No. I WANT to book a room next Monday.

Hotel: Oh, sorry. I understand! Please excuse me.

Then the hotelier hung up again. Hanoi is not yet ready to steal Hong Kong's crown for having the best hotel service in the world.

Crown jewels: Hong Kong private Mark Blacker was reading an editorial about the topless Fergie pictures scandal in the "Daily Inquirer", a newspaper from the Philippines.

This is what it said:

"Certainly, the present carryings-on among England's royalty, or their marital extensions, can't possibly remind the commoners of the glories of Elizabeth and Victoria. All they will remind them of is the incontinence of Henry VIII and its not very pleasant effects on barren women, or those incapable of bringing male offspring into the world."

Mark commented: "I knew Henry VIII had been accused of many dastardly deeds, but this personal revelation about his nocturnal habits breaks new ground in the release of historical information, not to mention its effect on the promotion of family planning techniques."

We find the whole thing baffling. Could Henry not have removed his incontinence garment if he was so desperate to father children?

Two Dicks: Writer Simon Winchester told us about an incident which took place in London recently.

An Englishman called Richard Stratton was visiting a Japanese advertising agency man.

The Japanese gentleman had become more English than the English.

His suit was by Huntsman. His shirt was by Harvie and Hudson. His tie was by Sulka. His shoes were by Church. And he had the most impeccable upper class English accent.

"My name's Richard Stratton," said Richard.

"Ew, Richard," said the Japanese chap. "May I call you Bob?"

SMART MACHINES AND SMART-ALEC MACHINES

WARNING: Do not read this article in the presence of the following items: digital diaries, tone-dial phones, computers, digital clocks or data-pagers. They may be reading over your shoulder.

Got away from them? Right. Without wanting to sound in the least bit paranoid, I would just like to point out all these blasted items are out to get me.

It all started when someone gave me a new Japanese alarm clock. Called a "trick alarm clock", it is designed to tease its owner awake. The face of the clock tells the correct time. The voice may or may not.

I set the thing to wake me at 7.30 am. There I am, fast asleep, when I hear a little synthetic voice. It says: "The. Time. Is. 8.15 . . . *MAYBE.*"

The shock of hearing a machine on which one depends, blatantly telling vicious porkie pies, is so great that one's mind becomes immediately alert with a kind of horror.

But there's another problem: I tend to deliberately set clocks a quarter or a half an hour early anyway, to help me get a head start. As a result, after a few days, neither me nor the clock has the faintest idea what time it is, or even what our own names are.

It is clear that my relationship with this device will be violent and of short duration.

At the newspaper office where I work, I spend much of my time on the telephone. Every so often, I find myself conversing with a voice-mail machine.

But these machines often ignore anyone using an old pulse-signal phone, like mine. They think only tone-phone users are of sufficient class to warrant attention.

Voice-Mail: Please press seven to leave a message.
(Pause.)
Voice-Mail: Please press seven to leave a message.
Me: I HAVE pressed @#$%¢*! button seven.
Voice-Mail: Please press seven to leave a message.
Me: I AM pressing it, you ¢%@#$!¢& idiotic machine.
Voice-Mail: This call is being terminated. Thank you for calling.
Me: Take that! And that! AND that!

Gratuitous acts of violence against telephone handsets are an excellent way of releasing tension, and I strongly recommend them to all readers.

There used to be a skyscraper which proclaimed itself as "The Most Intelligent Building in Hong Kong". When floor numbers were mounted on the outside, the number 15 was only three flights above the number 10. Most kindergarten classrooms are more intelligent than that.

A friend of mine works in a building with a "learning lift". This lift does not wait on the ground floor when unused. It is designed to "learn" where it is most requested at various times of day, and then loiter with intent around those floors at those times. For example, it should hover at the floor containing the secretarial pool at 5.30 pm, because that is when the secretaries go home.

But he has become convinced that it has maliciously decided to do the opposite. "Whenever I approach, it rushes away from me to the opposite end of the lift shaft. I think it has started to avoid humans, because we mean so much work for it," he said.

It will not take long for intelligent readers like yourself to realise what is really happening. Machines, after having achieved the ability to make logical computations, are moving onto the next stage: they are developing the ability to out-smart us. In some cases, this is not difficult.

The only hi-tech object I ever felt any affinity for was a timepiece made by Limax Co, a Taiwanese firm. It drinks Diet Coke. You just dribble the stuff in. No other power source is necessary. "It also works on coffee, scotch and wine," a spokeswoman told me.

I immediately felt enormous spiritual kinship with the object, having the same taste in fuel. I find I have to build up a sense of trust with machines these days. The few which are not out to get me, anyway.

TRUE STORIES

Proof that some people have too much money and should be forcibly deprived of it: A romantic couple (let's call them Mr and Mrs Lovebird) were staying at the Mandarin Oriental hotel in Hong Kong when there was an urgent phone call for the gentleman. It was from his office in the United States, summoning him back immediately for a board meeting.

Mrs Lovebird would have to return alone later. "I hate flying by myself," she sniffed.

So just before Mr Lovebird left, he hatched a cunning plan with the hotel concierge. The concierge went out and bought a substitute cuddly hubby — a six foot tall teddy bear.

The hotel man then secretly phoned the airline and reserved a seat next to Mrs Lovebird's seat, buying a first class ticket under the name "Mr T. Bear."

When the day of Mrs Lovebird's departure came, the concierge secretly heaved Mr T. Bear into his arms and headed off down to the check-in at Kai Tak airport (the things you do for love).

Unfortunately, the plan came unstuck.

The conspirators had completely forgotten that airline officials have their senses of humour surgically removed at birth.

They peered suspiciously at Mr T. Bear and demanded to see his passport.

The concierge explained that Mr T. Bear was not, in fact, a human being, and thus did not have a passport. It is one of those inexplicable truisms of life that stuffed toys often don't.

"Well, he can't get on the plane then," said the officials.

The hotel man was, however, allowed to place a magnum of champagne on the seat. (Bottles are apparently recognised as non-human, whereas teddy bears are a grey area.)

Mr Bear was eventually allowed to fly, but only in the cargo hold.

Mrs Lovebird was left alone in first class, quizzically looking at the champagne next to her, which came with a note: "From Mr T. Bear".

Didn't she get a surprise at the luggage carousel.

Moving story: Speeding along Gloucester Road, Hong Kong, we spotted a removal van. This was one of those yellow and red wood-framed trucks, emblazoned with the name Chung Wah Transportation Co.

As it drove in front of us, we could see that its cargo was a pair of metal executive desks and swivel chairs.

In one of the chairs a woman was fast asleep.

In the other, a man was sitting straight up and talking rapidly into a mobile phone.

Chung Wah Transportation: the removal firm that shifts your office furniture without your staff noticing.

Brief encounter: The impossible takes longer, except in Mongkok. A lawyer friend of ours in Central had his briefcase stolen while he was shopping. It contained his only set of keys to his Porsche 928S.

The lawyer, whom was shall call Perry Mason, contacted the Porsche dealers in Hong Kong. They told him he was in BIG trouble. There were only two options.

1. Go to Dusseldorf, Germany, with the number of the key and try to get a copy made by the Porsche factory.

2. Have the entire lock system removed from the car and replaced at a cost of HK$10,000.

Neither alternative made him throw his wig in the air with joy.

Then he had an idea. He and his colleagues had often defended an alleged car thief, whom they had always "got off". They decided to go and talk to him.

This much-suspected gentleman (although completely innocent of course) was shown the car and asked to get into it.

"He used something like a paper clip," Mr Mason said. "It only took him five minutes to break in."

The alleged car thief had a friend who was an, er, informal locksmith, so to speak.

"He took out the driver's side lock and disappeared off to Mongkok with it,' said the lawyer. An hour later, he came back with a set of keys.

Mr Mason broke the good news to a magistrate who had pledged to help trace and lock up the briefcase thief. "Ah. You seem to have solved this one by nipping over to the other side of the fence," commented the beak.

Health drink craze proves a tasteless wash-out: Do not read this item during breakfast.

People in Hong Kong have been consuming health

drinks — but not with their mouths. There's a mini-boom in an unexpected corner of the para-medical business in the territory.

A socialite revealed to us over lunch that she and large numbers of her peers go for "colonics" at Optimum Healthcare, a company in Causeway Bay which seems to have cornered this market.

Optimum Healthcare has had to keep its doors open until 8 pm on weekdays because of demand.

Without going into tasteless detail, let us say that colonics do for your colon what green rap group Public Enema hoped to do for Hong Kong's environment — clean it out from the inside.

The fashion among Hong Kong colonics fans is to consume some Barleygreen health drink. But they don't drink it. They have it, er, inserted.

Just think of all those food scientists spending months working on the taste of this drink, which is completely bypassing the taste buds.

Indecent exposure while One's namesake sleeps: Bert One woke suddenly, with an urgent need to rush to the bathroom. This was hardly surprising since he had spent a long night drinking in Wan Chai.

He staggered out of bed, trotted through the doorway and heard the door click shut behind him.

Then he noticed there was no toilet in the toilet. He was in the corridor. It is remarkable how quickly you can sober up when you are stark naked in a public place.

Bert One (that's his nickname) started hammering on the front door to wake his flatmate, Bert Two. But he knew it would be no use, since Bert Two was famous for his alcohol-induced comas.

Bert One, who revealed this tale to us yesterday, shuddered as he recalled the worst hours of his life.

After he had given up banging on the door, he tried to think of other possibilities. He was on the 11th floor of 375 Hennessy Road, an old tenement block. (He has since moved.) All his neighbours were elderly Chinese people.

He knocked on one door, which was eventually opened by an old Chinese woman. She screamed and slammed it shut.

Then someone called the police who arrived and found Bert still miserably clutching his undercarriage. They summoned the fire service.

The two forces made further attempts to revive Bert Two, including by telephone, to no avail. The firemen decided to smash down the door.

This noisy operation failed to awaken Bert Two, nor did hammering on his locked bedroom door.

In fact, Bert Two did not know anything about this event until the next day at 11 am, when he entered the living room and was heard to say: "What the @#%!'s happened to our front door?"

Dressing-down: In autumn last year, staff at Hong Kong radio channel Metro News asked their listeners to write in and give them feedback.

The Hunghom-based company expected letters from as far afield as Tsuen Wan, or even across the waters to distant Hong Kong island.

The last thing they expected was the letter from Azerbaijan that arrived. Apparently, people in that region with strong receivers can pick up Hong Kong broadcasting.

Three questions sprang to mind. Are the Azerbaijanis not rather busy struggling for independence? Why would they want to listen to 24-hour Hong Kong news station? What on earth do they make of Ted Marr?

Anyway, Metro staff were deeply touched by most of the long, handwritten letter, in which the writer asked for Metro radio souvenirs and photographs of the presenters.

Then came a second request: "My other favourite hobby is photos of nude Asian girls. Unfortunately, my collection is poor. My dream is to receive regularly such materials from Hong Kong. Could you send me something?"

Suddenly the letter's cuteness-factor diminished dramatically.

Metro spokesman Bob Palitz said: "We decided we could not really help him with this — we are a radio station, after all. But we are going to send him an audio cassette of nude Asian women."

We forecast crowds gathering at the Whampoa Gardens shopping centre for the taping session. The premises of Metro Broadcasting have glass walls.

Short trip: A business traveller called us on his way to the airport last night. His Cathay Pacific diary told him that a direct flight from Hong Kong to Los Angeles was 12,194 kilometres.

It also told him that a direct flight from Los Angeles to Hong Kong was only 12,082 km.

Where are the missing 112 kilometres? "Is it something to do with Los Angeles having a longer runway?" the traveller asked.

No. It's very simple. The extra kilometres clocked up when leaving Hong Kong is a phenomenon attributed to the fact that the territory is deep in the Twilight Zone.

Ruth-less response: Ruth Mitchell of Pak Sha Wan, Sai Kung, paid for some wine and arranged to have it delivered to her home. People who live off the beaten track know the potential difficulties in such situations, so she sent them a map.

That afternoon, she got an angry call from the delivery man.

Would you PLEASE open your door, he thundered. The delivery men are "outside your house NOW. Why you not answer?"

Ruth replied that there was no van of any kind outside her house, and the men must have gone to the wrong house.

"Not possible," was the reply. "We are outside your house NOW. You open door."

This unhelpful debate continued with both sides absolutely refusing to give ground.

Eventually, the caller said the men would no longer wait for her to open her door. Where would she like the wine left?

She said the wine should be left in the garden with the statue, near the palm tree.

You can guess the reply: "You have NO statue or palm tree in your garden!" They insisted that they were at the right house and she was wrong about her garden.

Meanwhile, in another part of the village, a HAECO night-shift worker eventually woke up to find a wine delivery company unloading boxes on his doorstep. He complained that there must be some mistake.

"They retorted that his house was the right one, and they had had enough," said Ruth.

What stands out about this tale is the stunning single-mindedness and determination of the delivery men in the face of huge odds.

Chris Patten may wish to get them on his side and appoint them to Legco.

I'll be 5 years late. They haven't built a road yet: An executive from International Computers Ltd recently started looking for staff for his airline computer project.

A young French lady who had recently arrived in Hong Kong applied for the job. They arranged the interview over the phone.

The man told the woman (let's call her Francoise) to come the following day to the ICL office at Kwo Tai Dai Ha.

"It's the building next to the airport on Concorde Road," he said.

The next morning Francois phoned and said she would be a bit late for her interview. The ICL executive said he would wait.

One hour later, she called again and apologised for a further delay, saying the journey was taking longer than she expected.

"It's okay," he replied. "I know what Hong Kong traffic is like."

Another hour passed. Finally, the young lady phoned again and said: "I'm at the airport now. But I can't find the building."

She explained that neither she nor the taxi driver could find ANY building, nor any road, nor in fact any sign of civilisation.

Had they driven off into another dimension?

No. Francoise had gone to the wrong airport. She had gone to that desolate patch of half-reclaimed landfill in a remote and inaccessible part of Lantau island, which is all that exists of Chek Lap Kok airport.

Another interview was arranged, and Francoise, perhaps surprisingly, got the job. The ICL executive was quite impressed.

"I have been here years, and I have no idea how to get to Chek Lap Kok," he said. "She's only been here for two months, and she got there, in less than half a day and on her own. If that is not efficiency and intelligence, I don't know what is."

Democracy makes great cents on streets of Taipei: The most sought-after purchase in Taiwan at the time of writing cannot be seen, cannot be touched and you can't take it home with you.

Yet people have been buying thousands of them, at NT$4,000 each — the equivalent of about HK$1,200.

That's what a vote costs. We heard this from David Symons, a Hong Kong businessman just returned from Taipei. "You can collect NT$4,000 from more than one candidate," he said.

Taiwan's central bank reckons that NT$20 billion was spent on the recent election, much of it to buy ethereal promises.

For David, one of the highlights of the election was when candidate Hsu Shao-tan, a 34-year-old former stripper, held a public meeting to denounce her critics, who were distributing a hard-core pornographic video of her.

The actress in the film had a mole on her breast, said Ms Hsu.

"But I do NOT!" she thundered, and ripped open her upper garments to make her points very clear.

But the award for financial manoeuvring must go to candidate Shih Kun-li.

The government offered a NT$10 million reward for anyone who caught a candidate buying votes.

Mr Shih, a taxi-driver, sold his friends some votes at NT$1 each, and then made a citizen's arrest of himself.

"If I get the reward, I'll be able to retire," he said.

Police were unsure how to react.

A little escapism: "Father Robbery" is not a common name for a clergyman.

But it happens to be the nickname of Discovery Bay vicar Rob Gillion, because his hobby is making armed raids on jewellery shops.

No, only joking. Rob, who has appeared in these columns before, has been given the label since he started spending time (voluntarily) at Shek Pik High Security Prison.

The prisoners always gave Rob bemused looks, and he soon found out why. Behind the prison gates, the designation for convicted robbers is "Rob". Since he is always pointed out as Rob, they assumed he really was "one of them".

Father Robbery recently organised a football match in the prison, and managed to get three of Hong Kong's best known footballers — Dale Tempest, Ross Greer and Iain Hesford — to play against the prisoners.

Ross and a prisoner both went to do headers and violently collided skulls. Unfortunately for Ross, the prisoner's name was Ironhead.

"Ironhead didn't feel a thing," said Father Robbery.

Then a ball from Iain went sailing up and over the barbed wire fence. You should have seen the amazing rush of volunteers clamouring to go and retrieve it.

"The match was a great success," said the clergyman. "So much so that the prisoners are hoping for another game soon — an away match."

Far far away.

Crown caught: A legal department crown counsel couldn't open his case — because he couldn't open his case. All the important papers concerning the first matter to be heard at 9.30 am at the High Court were in his briefcase.

But the lock had seized up, and there was no way to get into it.

Luckily, the suit, which was being heard before Mr Justice Leong, had to be adjourned for other reasons.

Of course, the lawyer could have just taken it into the

corridor and shouted: "Is there a lock-picker in the house?"

But there probably would not have been a great rush to admit it.

Voice matched: Now we wouldn't want to accuse Zambian tennis player Lighton Ndefwayl of being a sore loser, but this is what he said when he lost a match to his rival Musumba Bwayla (as quoted in New York's *Village Voice* recently and sent in by a Lai See reader):

"Musumba Bwayla is a stupid man and a hopeless player. He has a huge nose and is cross-eyed. Girls hate him. He beat me because my jockstrap was too tight and because when he serves, he farts, and that made me lose my concentration, for which I am famous throughout Zambia."

A big pest: Danny Ledoux is boss of Pesticides Services Co, the Hong Kong firm with the controversial slogan "Killing is our business".

People sometimes react oddly to it — particularly if they see the van from behind, where they can see the slogan but not the name of the firm.

Danny told us he once got a call from a woman in Hong Kong who had not realised that his expertise in killing referred to pest control.

"She asked me if I could send someone to do 'a job' for her in the Philippines," said Danny. "She wanted us to pay a visit to her husband."

Perotnistas: Reggie Bosman, native of Stanley, went down to the Marriott gift shop to buy a presidential candidate watch for his American-born wife shortly before the US election.

The glum *serveuse* volunteered the information that she had shifted only five since they had gone on sale.

Rather taken with them, Reg bought one of each presidential candidate at HK$180 and, donning the Clinton version, sprinted off to catch the 260 bus.

This bus happened to contain a load of Americans, who spotted Reg's Clinton-o-meter and were extremely interested.

On hearing the price was the equivalent of US$23, cries of "Gee" went up.

"But hold," cried Reg, and produced the other two models.

At the sight of the Perot-o-meter, the bus almost erupted.

"AAAAA-RIIIGHT!" said the Americans.

Hordes of them offered to buy all three watches at US$25 each. Like a true Hong Kong entrepreneur, Reg flogged the watches and pocketed the US$75.

"Why dincha buy more?" grumbled the rest of the crowd.

So Reg took a straw poll of how many more he could have sold on the bus.

He worked out that his takings for this bus journey alone would have been HK$3,510.

By the end of the bus journey, the new owner of the Perot-o-meter had sold it to a fellow tourist for US$30.

Reg has since sold watches on the bus several times.

"The Perot-o-meters are now sold out," he said.

Knight shirt: Sir Hugh Bidwell, who was Lord Mayor of London in 1989-90, was in Hong Kong. He and his henchmen have been on a trade mission to China, trying to persuade mainlanders to buy British.

"We sold the city of London. We have got a lot to be proud of. We have survived and prospered on international trade," he boasted proudly.

Sir Hugh was being interviewed by one of our reporters, when he had to cut the interview short because his tailor had arrived to measure him up for some shirts. "I always get my shirts in Hong Kong," he confided.

Dog-gone: There was a problem. Uncle Number Two in Vancouver had a passionate hankering for a traditional Chinese dish: dog meat.

And we don't mean meaty chunks for Fido. We mean meaty chunks OF Fido.

But those squeamish Canadians frown upon hungry immigrants who get stuck into domestic pets.

So the Hong Kong branch of the family bought a supply of tinned roast dog from China and smuggled it to Canada.

The transfer was successful: one can bypass import restrictions, since customs officers assume "dog meat" is meat for dogs.

We heard this from a contact at property firm Colliers Jardine, who introduced us to a mysterious chap called the Dognapper. He told us about the incident which gave him his nickname. His friends and he were dining at a restaurant near the pier on that island, when they heard a piteous whimpering coming from a drum.

They opened it to find a black puppy, trussed like a chicken, obviously ready for the pot.

"We offered to buy the puppy but the owner said 'no'," he said. So the Dognapper waited until the ferry from Peng Chau to Discovery Bay was just about to pull out.

Then a henchwoman distracted the restaurateur, and the Dognapper grabbed the puppy, ran out of the shop and leapt into the boat.

The extradited puppy was adopted by a family in Discovery Bay.

The dog's nickname is "Lunch".

Dog daze: John Dickey, boss of Hong Kong firm CA-Packard, was amazed at a front page story about HK$192,000 worth of dogs being stolen from a flat in Ap Lei Chau Main Street.

"That means that at one stage, in one Hong Kong residential flat, there were 24 dogs, five victims and two robbers," he said. "Must have been cosy."

In a recent Tai Kok Tsui robbery, 25 dogs were stolen from a single garage.

The embarrassing thing is that most of the dogs in these robberies are watchdogs.

What will be stolen next? Burglar alarms?

Where customers can go, and what they can do there: Robert Nield of Price Waterhouse was in the recently opened Shoegazine shoe shop in Prince's Building, Hong Kong.

There was background music seeping out of the walls as usual.

It was only after a little time passed that he began to listen closely to it.

What he heard was the rousing final chorus of the song, which went: "Thank you for f***ing at the f*** shop."

"I am not a prude, but I thought it a strange choice," said Robert. "Perhaps I had misheard."

But then the next track started.

"Boom. Boom. Bam. Get the f*** out. Get the f*** out," sang the boisterous group.

"At this point, I asked the young lady shop assistant if she realised what the words meant," said Robert.

She said she did, but she could not go and change the music, since there was a customer — Mr Nield himself — in the shop.

"I obliged her — and the singer on the tape — and left," said Robert.

Clearly this is one of those "explicit lyrics" rap albums

that are all the rage these days.

However, if there was a prize for the least suitable piece of music in the known universe to use as muzak to make a customer feel comfortable in a posh shop, it would go to a rap song called "Get the f*** out."

AND MOSES TOLD THEM TO TAKE SOME TABLETS

You will never have read a history of the world like the one sent to us by Robert Davison of the Department of Information Systems, Hong Kong City Polytechnic.

The text was originally compiled by a history and English teacher called Richard Lederer.

It is made up of genuine bloopers from school essays, and first appeared in 1992 in the *Society of College and University Planners Digest*.

Here's the gist of "The World According to Student Bloopers".

The inhabitants of ancient Egypt were called mummies. They lived in the Sarah Dessert and travelled by Camelot.

The climate of the Sarah is such that the inhabitants have to live elsewhere, so certain areas of the dessert are cultivated by irritation.

In the first book of the Bible, "Guinnesses", Adam and Eve were created from an apple tree. One of their children,

Cain, asked: "Am I my brother's son?" Jacob, son of Isaac, stole his brother's birth mark.

Moses went up on Mount Cyanide to get the Ten Commandments. David was a Hebrew king skilled at playing the liar. He fought with the Philatelists. Solomon, one of David's sons, had 500 wives and 500 porcupines.

Homer wrote the "Oddity", in which Penelope was the last hardship that Ulysses endured on his journey. Eventually the Ramons conquered the Greeks.

Then came the Middle Ages. King Alfred conquered the Dames. King Arthur lived in the Age of Shivery.

Another tale tells of William Tell, who shot an arrow through an apple while standing on his son's head.

Sir Francis Drake circumcised the world with a 100-foot clipper. Queen Elizabeth's navy went out and defeated the Spanish Armadillo.

William Shakespeare lived in Windsor with his merry wives, writing tragedies, comedies and errors.

Romeo and Juliet are an example of a heroic couplet.

Milton wrote "Paradise Lost". Then his wife died and he wrote "Paradise Regained".

Benjamin Franklin invented electricity by rubbing cats backwards. He declared: "A horse divided against itself cannot stand."

WHY COMPROMISE? GET DIVORCED INSTEAD

CHEN looked like he was about to burst into tears. "Three of my clients are in the throes of messy divorces," he said, sniffing. "And two others have this week started trial separations."

He dabbed his eyes with his handkerchief. "I'm SOOO happy," he exclaimed, emotionally. "Why is life so good to me?"

You think Chen is a divorce lawyer, right? Or a solicitor's tout? Well, he is not. He is a property agent. He rents out flats at exorbitant prices and takes a fat percentage.

But this evil genius has a wonderful get-rich-quick formula that cannot fail. He calls it the Slammed Doors Principle.

Statistics show that for every 100 married households that go through divorce, 153 dwellings will be needed. "That's an instant 53 per cent growth in the market," boasts Chen, which is not his real name.

For him personally, the figures are even better: he specialises in providing services to couples likely to argue. He can spot them a mile off.

"My best bets are self-centred young yuppies in the rapture of first love. They earn a bit of money and quickly move in together without much thought," he said.

Chen has studied the subject. In the UK alone, divorces are directly responsible for a demand for 80,000 new homes a year. A similar phenomenon is just starting in Asia, with a new generation of impetuous yuppies lining up to do the wrong thing with their partners. "Yuppies make the same mistakes as real people, but they make them more expensively," said the property agent.

Personally, I blame Hollywood for raising false expectations. In movieland, escapees from bad marriages are always whisked away to a fresh adventure by someone such as Dudley Moore or Kathleen Turner.

In real life only one in three divorced people find anyone at all to move in with straight away. And who is that person?

Statistics reveal the shocking fact that that person is almost always your mother. Well, not YOUR mother, but the individual concerned's mother, if you see what I mean. Of course, in the case of you, the reader, it would be YOUR mother.

This trend is particularly profitable in places such as Japan and Hong Kong, where a demand for ever-smaller pieces of birdcage-like accommodation is what the market caters for best.

Chen proudly points out that divorces have benefits (for him) that last for years. Splintered couples tend to go off and start new families. They then need larger homes to accommodate extra children visiting at weekends.

When I showed the first half of this essay to someone, she commented: "You should write that this property agent is a complete slimeball."

"I would," I replied. "But the editor dislikes tautology."

What worries me is that there is only one short step from profiting from the arguments of couples to actually interfering with relationships yourself.

Chen's biggest temptation, he admits, is to try to sow the seeds of discontent himself. I've seen him do it. This is the sort of thing that happens: a Yuplet and Yuplette in their early 20s come into his shop.

Yuplet: Have you got a one-bedroom flat in this area?

Chen: Certainly... (Nods in direction of Yuplette.) You're not thinking of moving in with her, are you?

Yuplet: (surprised) Yes. Why?

Chen: Oh, nothing, nothing. (Directs next question at Yuplette.) Are you sure you wouldn't prefer two bedrooms, you know, to have one spare?

Yuplette: We only need one bedroom.

(Chen restructures his cheek muscles and eyebrows to convey the silent message: if I could tell you half the things I know about this young man, you'd think differently.)

I asked Chen what he would do if all the couples on his book were unexpectedly getting on well for a long period of time, and not generating any new contracts.

"I might be tempted to stick my oar in," he said.

What precisely he meant by this phrase I did not wish to ask.

But I am going to be suspicious the next time he tells me he is spending the afternoon doing an in-depth probe into highly desirable places.

PEKING ORDER

Fishy tale: Joe Lung, boss of Dataquest Hong Kong, went on a business trip to Beijing. On arrival, he took a group of American friends to the new giant McDonald's outlet in the centre of the city.

As they settled in their seats with their burgers and fries, one of the Americans complained. "Hey. This isn't ketchup."

Close scrutiny of the little sachets handed out proved him correct. They were individual packets of Oil of Ulan hand cream.

No wonder the Filet O'Fish doesn't taste quite the same in Beijing!

No flies on us: There is no airborne insect life in the first class hotels of Beijing. This we learn from Lynn Grebstad, director of public relations at the Peninsula Group, who faxed us from the Palace Hotel in Beijing.

A report in the *Beijing Evening Post* said: "An inspection by Beijing Tourism Administration and the press proved that no flies exist in Beijing's major hotels.

"After checking hotel lobbies, restaurants, toilets, guest rooms and kitchens, staff canteens and garbage rooms, the inspection proved that the following hotels do not have any flies: the Palace Hotel, Novotel, Great Wall, Jianguo, Lido and Beijing-Toronto.

"However, flies are still 'at large' in Huifeng Restaurant, Tao Ran Hotel and Bai Le Hotel."

If you visit any of the upper class hotels in Beijing and find yourself bitten by something, it must be either your imagination or your companion. Kindly write a self-critical essay.

That's entertainment: Mike Purefoy of Pokfulam, Hong Kong, was taken to see an acrobatic show presented by the Ministry of Railways Acrobatic Troupe in Beijing.

He brought the programme home with him.

Fixing Car On High Table Performers: Liu Mei, Wang Jun-gwo, Li Xia.

Standing On Hands Performers: Xing Chang-shu, Wang De-shang.

Playing With Balls Performers: Yang Se-lai, Liu Yong-jun.

Juggling With Feet Performers: Yu Ming, Yu Hong.

Kicking Bowls Performers: Ma Lan-zhen, Wang Pei-wen.

Playing With Head Performers: Zhou Rui-wu, Zhu Rui-hua.

It makes you realise how different the concept of entertainment is on the other side of the big fence. That "Playing With Balls" sounds a bit avant-garde.

For pleasure and profit: Wayne Beer of Swiss-Sure Co accidentally received a stray fax from Kwan and Chow solicitors of Wellington Street, Hong Kong.

"Dear Sir," it said. "We refer to the Form TM-No.50 which has been signed by the Chairman and General Manager of Ningbo Jielier Children Making Co Ltd."

Children-making companies? We've never heard it called *that* before.

Steve follows the rising son: Hong Kong businessman Steve Temkin gritted his teeth as he realised what he had to achieve. Mission impossible: build up a personal rapport with top mainland banker Chen Yuan.

Mr Chen was due to fly into Shenzhen on the Wednesday, and Steve, who works for Hong Kong sports bag maker Pam and Frank Industrial, managed to pull enough strings to get onto his appointments list.

Mr Chen is head honcho at the People's Bank of China — but is also the son of Chen Yun, the second most powerful man in China and main man extraordinaire of the conservative wing of the Communist Party.

Then disaster struck.

Mr Chen's plane from Beijing had a few problems (hard to believe, we know) and touched down late in Shenzhen. Several time-slots, including his audience with Steve, were cancelled.

But the Hong Kong businessman learned that Mr Chen was going to a karaoke club in the eastern part of the city, and might be able to see him then.

Steve sped to the club and heard warbling sounds from a private room. He entered to find the bank chief in full song.

The next musical number which came up on the television screen was *Zai Yuzhong* (In the Rain), a syrupy Mandarin love song with the boy and the girl alternating incredibly drippy lines.

There were no women in the room — so Steve knew what had to do.

Yes. He grabbed the microphone and volunteered to take the female lover's part.

The music started.

"I left you in the rain," Steve crooned to Mr Chen.

"I kissed you goodbye in the rain," Mr Chen twittered to Steve.

They cooed.

They twittered.

They cast longing looks at each other.

The sports bag specialist thought to himself: "I'm singing a love song with a guy who called the Great Helmsman 'Uncle Mao'."

Anyway, suffice it to say that the joint love duet was a personal rapport beyond Steve's wildest dreams.

Any more of a personal rapport would probably have been illegal.

Blast it: Boffins in drought-struck Sichuan province, southwest China, have developed a new system for guaranteeing that it will rain at the right time.

They have a team of meteorologists watching for rainclouds. Then they shoot the clouds with anti-aircraft guns until they discharge the rain they hold.

More than 300 guns have been assembled around the province, says *Business Weekly*, published by the China Daily group.

"Gunners open fire when moisture-bearing clouds are located," says the report. "So far more than 4,000 artillery shells have been fired to encourage rain."

We hope they don't try this in Hong Kong after 1997. We would much rather just have the water shortage, thank you very much.

Airport Ups and downs: Shenzhen is coming along in leaps and bounds. Aircraft landing there may arrive in similar fashion.

Howard Banwell, vice-president of Citibank Hong Kong, has been studying the new airport there, the full name of which is Shenzhen Fuyong Airport. It sounds impressive.

"It can fly up and fall down any kinds of the large airplanes," says the official brochure.

At the moment it is a class 4E airport. "However, in the late period, it will construct another runway for international airplane raising and falling only."

International passengers will find the news comforting.

The unique terminology used by Shenzhen airport may cause problems when pilots call air traffic control.

Pilot: Alpha Bravo calling. Are we clear to land?
Shenzhen Airport: We hope you fall down now.
Pilot: Charming.

Once you have landed in Shenzhen, what do you do? Head for one of the hot new capitalist-style clubs.

Toy maker Paul Hurlow showed us a brochure for a swanky Shenzhen establishment called Dynasty Club — no relation to the Hong Kong namesake. Its aim is to establish "closer and deeper communications between aliens and Chinese".

It offers a karaoke lounge with "quiet surrounding and hospital service".

Presumably this is for patching up damaged ear-drums. It will also be useful for people whose planes have fallen down.

Perfect harmony: China has a new tour agent. It is called

Supreme Harmony Travel Service, but is widely known as SHTS for obvious reasons (by which we mean that that is the acronym).

Anyway, the fuss about Tiananmen Square seems to have died down in the minds of people in the tourism business.

We say this because a recent issue of *Travel China* reports that SHTS has launched some military tours in Beijing. Tourists can have their pictures taken on tanks, practice shooting with PLA guns and so on.

We'd have thought that they would like to disassociate China and tanks in the minds of tourists, but then, they are the experts.

A friend of ours in Beijing says there is a rumour that an overseas branch of the agency is going to be set up, called Supreme Harmony International Travel Service, but he does not know what it will be called for short.

Smoke without fire: John Flynn of Millipore Asia, the satellite TV firm, told us about a revolutionary new way of solving the smoking/no-smoking dispute on airlines.

The new system is already in operation on CAAC flights between Beijing and Shanghai.

At the check-in desk in Beijing, he requested a no-smoking seat and he received a boarding card with the words "No Smoking" stamped on.

However, when the flight took off, the passengers sitting next to him were puffing away like moderate-sized Kuwaiti oilfields.

Mr Flynn summoned the stewardess through the fog and asked what was going on.

She explained that the flight did not have a non-smoking section as such. However, any individual seat could be designated a non-smoking seat.

All you have to do is ask for a non-smoking seat at check-in, and – hey presto – you are instantly not allowed to smoke in that seat.

"She politely added that I must not smoke, as my boarding card indicated I had a no-smoking seat," Mr Flynn said.

The only thing you achieve by asking for a non-smoking seat is to lose your right to smoke, should you be a non-smoker who suddenly has a dramatic change of heart, unlikely though it may sound.

Passive smoking is not something CAAC has considered. Nor, we suspect, is thinking, passive or otherwise.

Gut instinct: Private eyes from Pinkerton's detective agency in Hong Kong told us an exciting tale about a recent assignment they had been on in China.

The operation was a joint one, involving an officer from the mainland equivalent of the customs and excise authorities.

The team was hot on the trail of a consignment of posh designer label belts, which were actually cheap and nasty copies being sold by conmen.

At last they found the counterfeit goods! A whole box of them. They wrenched it open and pulled out the fake designer belts.

The belts seemed strangely familiar – then all eyes turned to the central portion of the mainland customs official, and they realised where they had seen one before.

Puff and the dragon: Dennis Levanthal and Bert Groenveld of Hong Kong-based SGS labs were in Ningbo on business. Bert went to the hotel shop for some cigarettes.

Bert: Do you have any Marlboro?

Salesgirl (helpfully): Yes sir. Would you like the short ones or the long ones?

Bert (thinks for a moment): The short ones, please.

Salesgirl (cheerfully): I'm sorry sir. We don't have any short ones.

Nice to have a choice, though.

Later, they found themselves at Shanghai Hongqiao Airport, which is now a heavily sign-posted no smoking area.

Bert, desperate for a nicotine fix, wandered off to find a spot to sneak a quick drag before take-off.

He found a virtually empty waiting area. As he puffed, he noticed a man in uniform watching him. When he had finished his cigarette, the guard strolled over and said it was illegal to smoke in the airport. But Bert could clear his liability by paying an on-the-spot fine of five foreign exchange certificates, to him, the guard.

Bert handed him a 10 FEC note.

The guard said he had no change.

"That's all right," said Bert. "I'm planning to have another cigarette before my flight. So I'm paying the second fine in advance."

Bert enjoyed a second cigarette at leisure, knowing he would be unmolested by the Shanghai authorities. It was probably the most enjoyable five FEC he'd ever spent.

MC^2: Scientific investigator Sheilah Hamilton recently went to a Beijing conference of international forensic scientists.

At a restaurant called Dingling on the outskirts of Beijing, she found the ladies' toilets had "WC" on them and the men's toilets had "MC" on them.

There's a kind of logic to it, if you think about it.

Needled: An increasing number of *gwailo* are making regular trips to Shenzhen now that business is booming there.

The second nastiest part of the experience is walking on

the bridge over the Shenzhen River (actually a huge, free-flowing toilet).

But the most infuriating thing about it is the horribly racist foreigners-only health check. People of Chinese race don't have to fill in a health form declaring they don't have AIDS. This is true even if they are promiscuous gay intravenous drug-users who have spent their whole lives juggling used syringes in Central Africa.

People of non-Chinese race are sternly waved over to the Health Quarantine Station. Westerners are not allowed through without filling in a AIDS health declaration — even if they are the Pope.

One American businessman friend, known as The Bagman of To Kwa Wan, noticed that little attention is paid to these forms, which ask you whether you have AIDS, leprosy or psychosis.

So he filled in his name as "Bill Clinton", and got through fine. If the real Mr Clinton ever makes a visit to Shenzhen, he will be surprised to find that according to the files, it is his second visit.

On other occasions, the Bagman has successfully presented himself as the Beatles (each in turn, including the deceased John Lennon), Richard Nixon, Joe Blow, Lord Wilson and so on.

"I went through yesterday as Chris Patten," said the Bagman when we called him. The only good thing that can be said about it is that the staff are trusting, and accept whatever you declare.

"Even if you were wheeled into the room in an oxygen tent with multiple intravenous hookups, as long as you say on the form that there is nothing wrong with you, they let you through," he said.

Issue of taste: A Cargolux plan from Singapore landed in

Shenzhen airport on a Sunday – the first international flight to do so. To celebrate, a Western-style buffet was laid out in the Window on the World restaurant in the terminal.

In attendance were some People's Liberation Army officers in green uniform. They strutted about, showing that they could handle a posh business function as well as any capitalist from Hong Kong.

We watched as one officer started at one end of the buffet and piled his plate high as he strolled along.

First came a layer of roast ham.

This was augmented by roast beef.

Then came a serving of potato salad.

Then a large slice of chocolate cake.

(All went on to the same plate.)

And over the top of the whole lot he poured a generous helping of thousand island dressing.

As he tried to eat the horrific result, you could see his opinion of Western cuisine plummeting with every mouthful.

Dead pan: In the latest issue of *Amcham*, there is a report about how American television shows are being bought and shown in Shanghai.

It says: "Among the few shows that were not approved by Chinese authorities is *The Postman Always Rings Twice* starring Jack Nicholson, because 'Murdering your husband is not good for the Chinese,' Cai Wenkui, director of advertising for Shanghai Broadcast, was quoted as saying by the *New York Times*."

So is murdering your husband considered great for *gweilo* marriages?

We recall the words of Commander G.H. Hatherill, a British policeman quoted in the *Observer* in 1954: "There are only about 20 murders a year in London and not all are serious — some are just husbands killing their wives."

Surgery awaits redundant organs: A major streamlining operation is being carried out by the National People's Congress.

The most penetrating description of this we have yet seen is in *China Market,* a journal published by Economic Information and Agency. Chris Duston of the ASM Group sent us his copy.

In it, Ah Zuo writes: "During my interview with Director Liu Yi of the State Tourism Bureau by the end of last year, I asked him whether his bureau would be disorganised.

"Liu said he had visited the office in charge of the size of government organs, which is located at 22 Xianmen Street. 'I asked people there whether my bureau would be disorganised. They said they were discussing matters concerning the disorganisation with people from units to be disorganised, but had no plan to discuss with me.'

"China had since 1948 cut back on the number of its government organs seven times."

Now we know why Chinese leaders have been in a bad mood lately.

Smoke signals: People in China don't have the same horror of smoking as people in the west. When the SAS Royal Hotel was opened in Beijing, staff chose English names for themselves, we heard from a reader in Beijing.

As a result, there is a young man named Marlboro there.

"He even wanted to print it on a name label in the same way that it is on the cigarette firm's trade mark," said our source.

There is also a Camel at the hotel.

Since one of the most popular Chinese family names is Lo, it would be easy for a Beijing smoker to call himself Lo

Tar.

No comeback: Richard Parry of the Regal Riverside Hotel picked up a copy of that essential magazine *Guangzhou Today*.

In it he found a rather backhanded compliment about the Yuexie District, in the shape of the following slogan: "People may enjoy themselves in these places so much as to forget to return."

Now that's what we call putting a positive spin on things.

Barbarians at the gate: Dennis Levanthal, director of the China division of SGS laboratory, was at Beijing airport in the waiting room attached to Gate 40.

It was a sweltering 31 degrees outside.

Inside, there were air-conditioners and fans, but the temperature was even hotter, since none of them was switched on, and all the windows and doors were kept firmly closed.

In other words, everything was pretty much as normal.

Or was it? After cleaning his glasses for the third time, Dennis realised that he was in a fast-thickening cloud of smoke.

Peering through the haze, he counted no less than seven people puffing away at cigarettes — all of them airport ground crew staff.

Also clearly visible were 15 "No Smoking" signs.

Dennis went to the service counter. He commented to the attendant on the number of "No Smoking" signs and the large number of people offending against this regulation.

She peered around. "That's okay," she said. "They're not passengers."

Please exit cabin before opening parachutes: Heard a revealing tale about the emergence of the package tour trade in

China from Mark Simon, Hong Kong-based shipping manager for Sealand.

A friend of his was on an internal flight in China recently.

As well as the usual business travellers and tourists, there was a party of elderly mainlanders. Although they were a tour group — they all had the same badges and were sitting in two rows in a back corner — they seemed unused to the conventions of international airlines. But they were very polite and obedient.

The video safety demonstration started rolling on the screen at the front of the cabin. The woman on the video said that in the event of an emergency, passengers should pull out the inflatable vest from under their seats.

The eight or nine members of the tour group immediately reached under their seats, tugged out the emergency vests and laboriously donned them.

The video stewardess continued: once you have left the plane, pull the little tag on the side to inflate the vest.

Members of the group yanked at the tags to inflate the vests.

The "live" stewardesses and seasoned travellers roared with laughter.

"Other passengers had to help them remove the vests," said Mark.

We suspect their mirth would have been short-lived had the passengers continued to follow the rest of the emergency procedures. Especially the bit about opening the plane doors and operating the fold-out emergency slide.

Smoke screen: Cigarettes in Hong Kong have a little paragraph of medical information on the side. Some packs of smokes sold in China also have a teeny paragraph of health information on the side.

The difference is that these packs from China are not

emblazoned with medical warnings — but with health recommendations.

Jin Jian filter cigarettes from Beijing Cigarette Factory have the following words printed on the front in English and Chinese: "It contains Chinese medicinal herbs, being new type and, therefore, safe to use."

A packet of Kezhi Ning smokes from Harbin Wan Long International Medicine Cigarette Co was sent to us by John Follansbee of The Home Insurance Co.

On the side of the packet in two languages are the following instructions:

"It is used for internal and mixed Hemorrhoids. 7-12 pieces of this cigarette should be smoked every day. During smoking this cigarette, abstain from wine and peppery food. Pregnant women are not allowed."

In other words, you should smoke at least 50 a week and avoid consorting with mums-to-be.

It is hard to picture how anyone could actually use these cigarettes for getting rid of hemorrhoids.

John said: "This gives new meaning to the Anglo-American joke which starts: 'Can I bum a cigarette?'"

Air of hope: Simon Kalen Chau of Power (JV) Co picked up a copy of "Hope", the in-flight magazine for China Southern Airlines.

"I took this magazine from my last, frightening, flight from Guizhou," he said. "We were there for a power station project. The pilots flew like jet fighter crew, and the landing seemed as if we were landing on rocks."

He tried to distract himself from his perilous situation by reading the magazine.

The first article he read was about the invention, development and history of the parachute.

The next one he looked at was headlined: "How Does A

Pilot Bale Out?"

We don't profess to know more about airlines than professionals, but are these really the most relaxing topics for nervous passengers to read about?

And why is the magazine called "Hope", anyway?

Only connect: Ram Sajnani of Reena Enterprises, a saree importer, went to Shenzhen for a long weekend. He popped into Hotel Honey Lake to meet his friend Vicky, who had checked in two days previously.

The receptionist told him to pick up the phone and ask the operator to be put through.

"Please wait," the operator told him.

After a few seconds, a woman approached Ram across the lobby and told him there was a phone call for him.

Yes, they had connected him with himself.

And be nice to the triads: they're patriots too: Many people in Hong Kong are concerned about the 10,000 People's Liberation Army soldiers due to be placed here in 1997. A group of business people, plus an academic, enlisted our help in composing a helpful leaflet for the newcomers.

For some inexplicable reason, this writer was the only participant willing to sign the resulting document.

Preparatory Guidelines For People's Liberation Army Soldiers Posted to Hong Kong.

1. Tanks should be driven on left side of Nathan Road on arrival. Do not point barrel at shopkeepers as an aid to bargaining.

2. Never ask for fish-balls in Mongkok.

3. Do not ask Sam the Tailor to make you a shiny double-breasted mohair version of your PLA uniform, unless you are a Major or higher rank.

4. Do not use bayonets to clear space in Mass Transit

Railway carriages or trams during rush hour.

5. Statue Square is not Tiananmen Square. You are not required to dress in plain clothes and harass people using it, but you may do so on a voluntary basis for practice.

6. A Coca-Cola in a Lan Kwai Fong bar costs three months' wages. Drink it slowly.

7. The Noon-Day Gun may not be used for shooting practice unless the passing boat belongs to Jardine Watertours.

8. Do not attempt to pursue students in your tank. Hongkong students do not ride bicycles. They drive BMWs.

9. Do not slip Legislative Council members bundles of renminbi and ask them to wangle a few privileges for you.

10. Do not steal any luxury car with a crown on the registration plate.

AT LAST, ASIANS ARE MAKING THEIR SHARE OF IMPORTANT TECHNOLOGICAL ADVANCES, LIKE WEARABLE VITAMINS

TODAY, you will be instructed on how to make a comfortable and aesthetically pleasing chair out of inexpensive and easy-to-obtain materials: your own body parts. (Note: All parts used are reusable for their former purposes afterwards.)

But first, we turn to an urgent matter. Did you remember to put on your medicines this morning? Wearable vitamins are an important new trend in Asia, and no one should miss out.

This is not a joke. While you are reading this, many people are pulling Japanese-made Vitamin C tights onto their legs, anxious to get their full quota of goodness in places other supplements cannot go. Had buzzing sounds in your ears recently? It could it be the sound of a million leg-pores munching into their daily portion of the sunshine vitamin.

Other people are wearing Korean-made "flavour" socks, impregnated with healthful nodules. This strikes us as a dangerous habit to get into. What if you throw a pair of socks into your mouth and start masticating vigorously, only to find that they are not flavour socks at all. They are actually a pair of socks you hid under the bed 18 months ago because the local durian-seller complained about the stink.

Then there are the deodorising blouses, worn in Tokyo, which zap your armpits throughout the day, causing your sweat to immediately retreat back into your body, to emerge later, who knows where?

In Beijing, buyers are lining up to buy an upper body garment for women. This, made by a firm called Moon God, is infused with a secret recipe of herbs and spices.

Says the advertisement: "The Moon God Brassiere soothes the liver, invigorates blood circulation, stops pain, regulates menstruation, eliminates toxins, prevents breast cancer and enlarges the breasts."

The success rate is 96.1 per cent, says the maker.

Method: You put it on, and keep it on day and night.

Warning: "Not for use by children under the age of 15." This is presumably because kids would look rather odd with miraculously enlarged breasts.

Not all the new generation Asian clothes are designed to make people feel better. There is at least one garment intended to make people around you feel much worse.

The Shijiazhuang Electrical Appliance Factory in China is churning out the Electric Vest, for ladies. If anyone tries to have unwarranted contact with a woman wearing one, the vest gives him a short, sharp shock. We can see this being particularly useful to females who have been wearing their Moon God upper body garment for too long.

It is good to see that we Asians are claiming our share of serious technological advances, although our new products have to go through the teething stage.

At a trade fair in Hong Kong recently, a hi-tech company

was showing off a device that enables your computer screen to "display more than two million colours simultaneously".

This sounds like a wonderful idea, except for one thing. I don't think there *are* two million colours. I've had a thorough look round, and I can only find about 40, even if I include ones like lemony-pinkish-fuschia.

A Japanese firm came out with a provocative concept recently: a solar-powered torch which only works in direct sunlight. We are sure the inventor meant well, but we can foresee problems. How do you see the beam when you are standing outdoors on a bright sunny day? Has he really thought this through?

Anyway, we were going to tell you about turning your lower limbs into a chair. The Nada Chair, which is made in Shenzhen, is described as "The World's First Frameless Chair", but it is more like a chair-less chair. It has no seat, back, legs or arms. It is really just a fabric harness. One bit goes round your back and the other bit links it to your knees. Locked into position, you become your own chair.

This strikes me as a concept worth extending to other fields. String a few together, and you could have a car-less car, or a bus-less bus, even.

The harness is quite comfortable, really. The only problem is that it's time for lunch, and I can't reach my socks.

DR DOOM'S ABBREVIATED TAIL OF WOE

November 5, 1992: The sun was shining, the Hang Seng Index was moving steadily upwards, and turnover was running at a heady billion dollars an hour. Stockbrokers went gaily about their tasks, a skip in their step, a song in their hearts, and enzymes gushing from their mouths.

All except one.

Marc "Dr Doom" Faber was sitting in Faces restaurant in Citibank Plaza, with the table covered in charts, tables and research documents.

"It's a trap," he warned. "The Hang Seng is going to plummet. People think it's a rising market, but it has actually topped out."

"Yes, yes, we've heard that one before," we scoffed.

The eccentric moneyman said he was so sure about this that he would bet anything – including his precious ponytail.

Dr Faber vowed that he would cut off one centimetre of

his tresses for every 50 points the Hang Seng Index went up, starting today.

Since some specialists have predicted it will reach 7,200 within six months, he stands to lose his entire ponytail, which is about 12 cm long.

What if it went up further?

"Then I'll have to cut something else off," he said. "Perhaps your readers could nominate something."

Meanwhile, his rivals in the investment advice business told us last night that the Hang Seng Index could be moved up 50 points on a single biggish news break on Hutchison or HSBC.

The phones will be running hot this morning.

The following day: At 10 am today, the share market opened and the Hang Seng Index went steadily upwards. Marc Faber's spirits went steadily downwards.

Mid-way through the morning it rose more than 50 points, reaching 6,401.

Gotcha. We sharpened our scissors and prepared to head to his office in New World Tower.

But the ponytailed one must have worked some strange magic, because the market suddenly turned around and fell all day, finishing 32 points down.

Foiled again.

Several readers made suggestions about what Dr Faber could cut off when his ponytail has gone.

The only printable one came from Nigel Reid of Ernst and Young.

"I think he should cut off all contact with the Hong Kong stock market for one week. He'll have to go and sit in a dark room with no *Business Post*," he said.

No *Business Post?* There is such a thing as Human Rights, you know, Nige.

The following week: The gross schizophrenia of the Hang Seng Index has made our bet with Dr Doom hard to follow on both sides.

The investment adviser seemed to have correctly predicted the turn, since the market promptly headed in the opposite direction. But everything changed by Thursday this week, when the market closed at 6,447 − definitely 50 points up.

Dr Doom made an appointment for a 1 cm cut. As his tresses fell, so did the index − by 80 points. A little slower in meeting his promise, and he would have saved both the hair on his head and the HK$300 he paid Andre Norman for the unwanted trim.

"It was the most expensive centimetre I've ever had cut," he said doomily.

A few days later: Not everyone has been miserable about the plunging Hong Kong share market of the past three days. Deep sighs of relief have been heard from a hotel bedroom in Palm Beach, Florida.

This is the site of the Templeton Global Conference, and one of the speakers is a certain pony-tailed financier from Hong Kong.

"I slept very well," said Dr Faber. "Some very important chart points have decisively broken. A close below 6,000 will almost certainly seal the fate of the market."

As he said this, the market plunged below 6,000.

"I am greatly relieved that my pony-tail will remain intact," he gloated.

If Zhu Rongji is reading this, *please* make up with Chris Patten.

The following month: Turned on our Bloomberg stock market screen to watch the horror. The wounded Hang Seng

Index had dropped 411 points. In Cantonese numerology this signifies *"death, no doubt, no doubt."*

This cheery message did nothing for our appetite for lunch.

All our poor friends in the investment community must be in utter suicidal misery, we thought. Just at that moment, the phone rang. "Hi! How are you?" said the cheery voice of Marc "Dr Doom" Faber.

His timing has proved almost perfect. He lost only one centimetre of his ponytail before the market turned and fell.

"I took some of those special 101 brand Chinese pills, which made my hair grow back," said Dr Faber, calling from the Businessweek conference at the Regent hotel.

Three months later: At last. The real cause of the Sino-British row has been revealed. It is all the fault of the cunning Marc Faber, Hong Kong investment adviser. Every time the market reaches the level at which he has to fulfil his hair-cutting pledge, disaster strikes.

"The time has come to recognise the existence of the Faber Threshold," said a financial specialist yesterday.

We caught Marc Faber, ponytail swinging, packing his bags to head off on a research trip to Brazil.

"Okay, okay, I admit it. It is all me," he said. "When the market reached 6,400 I went to Wong Tai Sin Temple and gave a donation. I then told my good friend Chris Patten to gazette the reform bill, and I sent a fax to Li Peng, telling him what to say in his speech at the National People's Congress."

Dr Faber said he would need to resort to subterfuge less and less often.

"The market has reached what technical analysts call a Broadening Top, which is a very negative sign."

If he is wrong, the bald patch on his head may also become a Broadening Top.

MISPRUNTS

Hands off: Journalist David Fox saw a sign on a lift in the Lon Kwo Building, Chai Wan, Hong Kong:
If the lift breaks down, please do not handle yourself.
David said: "I'm sure most people can find some other way to pass the time."

Most pampered shopfront: Got a letter from Taipei-based China Airlines in Taiwan. "Dear Gold card member," it said. "We here at China Airlines dedicate ourselves to make your trips a most pleasant one for 'WE TREASURE EACH COUNTER'."
Can't say we've noticed that their counters are any better maintained than those of other airlines, have you?

Santa Louse: Sandra Brown of High West, Pokfulam, was shopping at UNY in Taikoo Shing, Hong Kong, just before Christmas when she came upon a most abusive sign in the soft toys department.

"STUFF SANTA CLAUSE" it said.

Clearly somebody had had it up to here with Christmas.

Get it write: Banish errors from your writing forever with an automatic proofreader. That's the enticing promise from Hong Kong software distributor Kenfil.

Featured in the latest edition of trade magazine *Kenfil News* is a clever piece of software called Grammatik Windows, which proofreads your work to provide completely error-free text.

"Grammatik proofreads your writing for thousands of writing errors. It gives you immediate, on-screen feedback on mistakes in grammer [sic], style, improper sentance [sic] construction," it says.

It will spot "Grammer [sic] and style errors" such as "Incorrent [sic] Verb Forms" and "Infintive [sic] usage". But you need "1 MB extented [sic] memory".

The rest of the magazine is much the same.

If this gear is so great, why don't the people at Kenfil use it themselves?

Top video expert: Got the latest meet-the-staff leaflet from KPS Video Express, Hong Kong. This features the beautiful Joanne of KPS Central, described as the 13th in a series of "KPS VIDEO EXPRESS EXPERTS".

Her favourite videos, it says, are *Faulty Towers* (sic) and *Monthly Python* (sic).

Best video synopsis: Hugh Chambers of Hong Kong Telecom was studying the advance material sent out to potential advertisers by TVB. This is from the synopsis of *Moby Dick,* on February 29: "When Ahab finally sights the huge Moby Dick, he steers his ship right for the whale. In a

desperate effort to escape, the whale capsizes."
Don't remember THAT happening in the book.

Touching advice: Richard Gardener of Shouson Hill Road tells us the Hong Kong School of Motoring in Wong Chuk Hang now does tests using a touch-screen computer. His son Andrew, taking a test, was handed an "Important Notice".

"Candidate is required to answer each question by touching the appropriate area on the screen with his/her figure only," it said.

It must be a way to test a candidate's general dexterity.

Positive test: Received a promotional document from STAR TV about the MTV channel. It said: "Presented by a team of personality VJs drawn from the region and further afield, the daily playlist is geared specifically to Asian testes."

Being an Asian male, and having watched five minutes of female dancers gyrating on MTV, we can confirm this is true.

Take three: Received a press release from public relations firm Rowland Company entitled "Rowland Strengthens Asia Pacific Management".

The last phrase in the second paragraph was the distinctly ungrammatical "who in Sydney".

Then we received another announcement, entitled "Erratum re: Rowland Strengthens Asia Pacific Management press release".

This said: "The last pharse (sic) in the 2nd paragraph should read 'who based in Sydney'."

That an improvement? Why Rowland no verbs? Rowland dumb.

Truth in advertising: Hong Kong businessman Thomas Wong had to pay 60 FEC as a departure tax from Nanjing Airport. He was handed a receipt which said it was: "Levied by the eivil Aviation Administration of China."

They have spelt "Evil" incorrectly.

Nevertheless, the group does seem to be revealing an impressively frank admission of its fundamental nature.

Stalled: Businesses in Beijing wound down to watch the Olympic swimming, a caller from that city told us. He said that the *China Daily's* Beijing Supplement was reporting that even the watermelon pedlar on *Huixindongjie* had stopped attending to customers.

The paper said: "He was too busy watching the miraculous diving of Fu Mingxia to pay attention to his own piddling business."

The Beijing man commented: "This seems unnecessarily condescending. The stall is quite big."

Out of place: Raghu Ram of Asian Sources Media Group was sent an announcement by Headway Trade Fairs. It listed the countries from which visitors attended recent Headway trade fairs in Hong Kong.

The list includes: "Normay", "Omen", and "Sandi Arabia".

Which planet are they on?

Cut-off: Many firms evidently do their translation work straight from a dictionary. This can produce fascinating results.

Pat MacLachlan was baffled by the instruction "Rush fiercely along the periods" which came on a piece of paper from Taiwan.

Then it clicked.

"Tear along the dotted line."

Floored: Jon Dean, a long-staying guest at the China Merchant Hotel in Hong Kong, returned home to be greeted by an assistant manager. The staff member suggested that Mr Dean and his wife change floors, because of a revolution scheduled to take place in 10 days' time.

"How thoughtful of him to share some inside rebel information with me," thought Mr Dean, rushing off to pack.

Further investigation revealed that the staff defined a revolution as the noun corresponding to the infinitive "to renovate".

Scariest vegetable: Displayed in the Park'N Shop at Austin Avenue, Kowloon: "VIOLENT EGGPLANT".

This follows close on the heels of reports about robbers in the UK using cucumbers and bananas in hold-ups.

Theory: police chief Li Kwan-ha has asked Park'N Shop to promote the cosh-shaped vegetable as a weapon, in order to lower the number of shoot-outs in jewellery raids in Tsim Sha Tsui.

Way of livings: A wonderful new Hong Kong social club has been set up in Wan Chai called "Oasists: Quality Life Explorers". It costs HK$1,480 to join, although the first 100 people to sign up will get in free. The brochure lists a large number of activities and interests on offer. These include:
Wines and Dines
Audios and Visuals
Thoughts and Thinkings
Self and Selves
Livies and Livings
Wears and Dresses
Traditions and Believes

These and Those
Sound really enticing, don't they? We're signing up. After all, you only livie once.

In practice: Ann Williams of Lockhart Road, Wan Chai, was reading the Hong Kong Arts Centre magazine.

This informs readers that they can learn how to draw the unclothed human figure at sessions in the "Loins Practice Room".

Is this a misprint for "Lions", or do they repeatedly draw the interesting bits only?

Fowl year ahead: This year, as we all know, is the Year of the Cock.

But in a classic piece of Victorian prudishness, almost everyone is opting for alternative terms, such as rooster, cockerel or chicken.

The sole exceptions, as far as we have seen, are the Post Office, which has bravely insisted on "Year of the Cock" on all its stamps, and British Airways, which is sending Year of the Cock cards.

Then there is Ready Mixed Concrete of Hung Hom, Kowloon, who wrote to its customers:

"Dear customers,

May we take this opportunity to wish you a Happy New Year of Cock."

Smoke signal: Got a press release from the Omni Marco Polo Hotel in Hong Kong saying that some unknown singer had been staying there.

Then we received a second one, which said:

"Apology: The name of the singer should be Mr Georgie Fame instead of Mr George Fume."

We rather like the name George Fume.

Perhaps the Hong Kong Tobacco Institute could market a singer by that name in their fight against the anti-smoking lobby?

Signing off: Nissen Davis of McDonnell Douglas Hong Kong saw on a door in an aircraft from a South Pacific regional airline:
EMERGENCY EXIT
Crew Use Only
This he saw at a car factory in Southern California:
EMERGENCY EXIT
Not to be used under any circumstances.

Alarming: Tony Banham of Infomix Software, Wan Chai, used to work in an office the door of which had a sign which said:
After Office Hours This Door Becomes Alarmed.
He was recently mulling over a large plastic bag marked with the words: "Keep Away From Children."
"It reminds you of just how dangerous children are," he remarked approvingly.

Problem palates: The Waterside Inn in Discovery Bay, Lantau, is sending out invitations to people to "Come and join us for our First Insular Wine-Tasting".
We always thought insular meant "inward-looking".
First wine-taster: I quite like this wine.
Second wine-taster: Who cares? Look, I've got my own problems, right?

Innovative: Writer David Chappell nipped into that posh shoeshop Sabato and Dominica, in Taikoo Shing, Hong Kong, and noticed a sign in the shop which says: "Please Try On Carpet'.

"I thought about it, but decided I would stick to the Persian silk rugs I usually wear," he said.

Pretty vacant: Ignatius Chan of Iguana Promotions Ltd, Conduit Road, Hong Kong, was driving through Central when he noticed an unusual message in neon lights on top of the Mandarin Oriental Hotel.

It said: "MAN IN ORIENTAL".

Boy, these low occupancy problems are getting serious.

Off the wall: Lorraine Little of Cahners Asia arrived back in Hong Kong after a long flight from Toronto. She needed to use the loo at Kai Tak airport.

"As I sat poised on the porcelain throne, I read a sign on the door," she told us.

Save Paper.
Use the hot air dryers.

How does one get the hot air dryers off the wall and into the cubicle?

Evil designs: Spotted a gentleman hawker selling neckties on the Tsim Sha Tsui side of the Star Ferry in Hong Kong.

Sick ties: HK$39, said the sign.

At first we thought "Sick" was a misprint for "Silk".

Then we caught sight of the patterns.

Hear hear: Spotted in Hong Kong Cityplaza shopping centre: a special offer in an earring shop.

Buy one, get one free.

This must be aimed at people who have two ears.

Special offer: Everett Krohn of the Krohn Collection, Duddell Street, Hong Kong, noticed a sign in the window of the handbag shop on Kai Chiu Street in Causeway Bay.

BUY ONE
GET ONE
Not very generous, are they?

Still fuming: Alan Jones of Intervisual Advertising, Wan Chai, was in the back of a Hong Kong taxi with "no smoking" signs all over the place.

About two minutes into the ride, the driver lit a cigarette.

"Being a smoker myself, I asked the driver if I could borrow his lighter to light my cigarette," said Alan.

The driver turned around, glared at Alan as if he (Alan) was completely mad, and pointed to the sticker on the back of the front seat.

"NO SMOKING!" he thundered.

Street smart: Spotted a scene in Tsim Sha Tsui which convinced us that there is some honesty among Kowloon merchants. Most of the hawkers were selling printed satin ties with signs saying "Real Silk".

But one chap was selling his ties with a sign saying "Guaranteed realistic". Much closer to the truth.

Price war: Sheung Wan-based writer Gerry O'Kane has just returned from Macau. He noted that a clothes shop in the Leal Senado district of the enclave has put a sign up in its window:

"SALE

"UP 50%".

Innovative sales technique.

Airless driver: Kim Urquhart of Hong Kong came upon a large, green hazardous materials truck on the main road in Tseung Kwan O.

The sign on the back said: "Do Not Inhale."

Surely if one obeys this dictum, there are other dangers, such as asphyxiating oneself?

Fun nighty out: Perfume trader Sham Navani was looking intrigued at a sign on the outside of the BBQ restaurant in Kimberly Road, Tsim Sha Tsui.

"Nighty open," it said.

We have heard of all sorts of kinky themes, but gaping sleep-wear is new.

Bristols fashion: Andrew Windebank of the Hongkong Automobile Association was peering quizzically at the window of the nightclub at the corner of Mody Road and Minden Avenue, Kowloon.

"The Four Sisters Topless Bar and Nightclub" said the sign. "No cover charge."

"I should think not," he said.

Hacked off: Public relations man Simon Clennell of Rowland Co has been scouting in the area around his office in Lyndhurst Terrace, Hong Kong, for places to take his clients.

The Tin Yin Vegetarian Restaurant in Lyndhurst Terrace has a notice on the window saying:

PLEASE DO NOT BRING ANY MEAT OR ALCOHOLIC INTO THESE PREMISES.

Simon found this rather disconcerting. "Could make it difficult when I'm trying to do my job of entertaining journalists."

***Almost* never:** Simon Clennell of Rowland Co is still scouting for places in Central to take clients. He came across the Ashoka Indian Restaurant in Wyndham Street.

This has a notice outside saying:

"WE NEVER CLOSE!
"Business Hours:
"12.00 – 2.30 pm
"6.00 – 10.30 pm."

Baby bloomer: David Gosling of Avon, Lippo Centre, Hong Kong, spotted a flower shop in Admiralty selling: "12 ROSES and BABYBETH" for HK$600.
What does Beth's mother have to say about this?

HOME SWEET HOTEL

A 5-Star Hotel
Hong Kong

In three days and four hours time, I will go back to living life in my apartment. And I will be as helpless as a flat-fish in traction at a basketball audition.

This is the Lament of the Long-Staying Hotel Guest Who is About to Return Home, and it is becoming an increasingly common complaint.

At home, I will expect my bed to be made up, turned down, and so on, at the proper times. But ugh: I will discover that the sheets are the SAME ONES I used the previous night. When hunger pangs strike, I'll discover there's no bell to summon room service, with its steaming trays of haute cuisine.

On entering the bathroom, I shall be outraged by the fact that yesterday's damp towels are still clinging to the rails.

Why, no one has even bothered to fold the end of my toilet roll into a triangle! How can a man live like this?

Hotel life may not be real life, but it is very easy to get used to.

Hostelries around Asia are frantically promoting long-stay packages to boost revenue in this lean period.

These are designed for business visitors setting up a complex deal. But they also suit the chronic sufferer of terminal laziness, the plight of the present writer.

At the time of writing, I shall have been living in an upper-class hotel for almost a month. I hereby offer to share my findings about the long-term effects of excessive high-living on the average human being.

First, the two best things.

1. Ten clean towels a day.

Boy, did Leona Helmsley know what decadence was all about.

Being in a double room, staff every day provided me with two hand towels, two face towels, two hair towels, two bathsheets, and two floor towels. I thought about asking for a back-of-the-knees towel (I have sweaty kneebacks) but didn't want them to think I was hard to please.

2. Clean white sheets every day (especially if they are linen) and the fact that the beds are made properly, with all the bits tucked in and the wrinkles smoothed out.

Now come on, admit it, how many of you actually go to the trouble of making your beds properly every morning? You just give the duvet a perfunctory shake to get the food out of the creases, like me, don't you? Last year, I found a mince pie in my bed TWO DAYS after Christmas. True.

The disadvantages, however, occur on a much more subtle level, and only become noticeable after at least three weeks. Here are the two worst things:

1. Hotels are unsuited to satisfying those little cravings

that hit you through the day.

You know the sort of thing I mean. In the middle of the morning, one needs a little something from the biscuit tin or your mother's cake box to go with your coffee. When you come home from work, you feel like scoffing a cold sausage from the back of the fridge. Late in the evening, you just want to put your nose into the fridge and grab something to eat while standing over the kitchen sink.

Well, you can't do any of the above at a hotel. You either order a whole meal from room service menu, or you go hungry.

The result, in my case, was that I ordered five meals a day.

Even worse, since room service menus are always exorbitantly priced, you feel obliged to eat everything on the tray, including all the condiments and a major proportion of the contents of the salt and pepper shakers.

2. The other awful thing is that you feel as if you are on show.

Every single day, strangers troop into your room, and perform vital operations — such as folding the end of your toilet roll into a little triangle.

Since one is always aware of this, one tends to be on one's best behaviour. The books on my bedside table have been Booker Prize winners throughout the past three weeks. No trash or porn that would give the chambermaids an opportunity to sneer at me.

Also, my underwear and pyjamas are always neatly folded and tucked away, so that they never see them. This is enormously uncharacteristic of me, as my wife will tell you, and a great cause of personal stress.

And you know those weekends when you want to throw off all your clothes, refuse to shave or pick anything up, and just vegetate in front of the television? Not possible. If you keep the Do Not Disturb sign on your door for more than half a day, they start to get suspicious and phone you up.

Anyway, for anyone reading this who is on his or her way to an extended stay at a hotel, here is a small but useful tip for keeping yourself up in the right frame of mind.

Any time you get fed up with it, just stroll to the window and watch the man/women-on-the-street slouch past. Notice that most of them are enviously looking in.

Have a good gloat at all those poor suckers who are going to have to go home and cook their own dinners. Clean their own baths. Dry their skinny bodies with used, damp towels which smell organic.

Five minutes of contemplating this and you feel wonderful.

But if I may go all philosophical for a moment, I must say that there is one enormous benefit to going home that outweighs all the delights of the high class hotel life.

My wife never loiters by the door looking embarrassed if I forget to give her a tip.

ALARMING DEVICES

PERSONALLY, we like our inanimate objects inanimate. So it was rather discomforting to stroll through the world's biggest watch fair and find it full of anthropomorphic gadgets.

Hong Kong is timepiece capital of the world. But the talking clocks on show at the convention centre in Wan Chai, are rather on the precocious side, with some proudly reciting the day of the week, date and month. Several firms offered desk calculators that recite whatever they find on their screens.

The Union Electric Corp had taught its digital watches to talk, which they do in English, Mandarin, French, Spanish and so on. Boss John Yu showed us the firm's ball-point pens, also given to chatter.

The one anthropomorphic gadget we really liked was the VSS20 alarm clock, made by Saitek of Hong Kong. It does not speak — but it does listen.

Picture the scene:

It is 7 am. The alarm goes off. You wake up and say: "AWW SHUDDAP!" (or words to that effect).

The alarm obediently shuts off. Four minutes later, it tries to wake you again, a little louder.

"GO BACK TO SLEEP," you snarl.

It shuts up again. Four minutes later it has another try.

"BUGGER OFF!" you say.

Once the alarm has let itself be delayed by eight verbal commands, it will ignore your abuse.

Sexiest alarm clock: This is from *Voice of ATV*, the staff newsletter of the Hong Kong television station:

TOSS-IT-OFF ALARM CLOCK.

The Staff Welfare Committee now offers a nice companion to the heavy sleepers — the Toss-It-Off alarm clock.

When the alarm clock rings, just toss it and it will stop ringing.

This miraculous device is available to ATV staff for only HK$38.

Don't complain to us. We don't make this stuff up. We just report it.

Cuckoo clock: Eric Spain of Avitel, Hong Kong, showed us the perfect clock for someone who is grumpy in the morning.

(If we don't get 14 hours sleep a night, we are grouchy all day. Come to think of it, we never get 14 hours.)

The clock is called the Wallbanger, and the packaging says it was "invented by a psychiatrist".

It is a small, pyramid-shaped clock dominated by a massive ball-shaped alarm which sits on top. In the morning, it rings like any normal alarm clock. These are the instructions:

1. When the dreaded time comes, the clock sends a signal to the ball and the alarm sounds.

2. Now it's fun time! Turn over and grab the ball off the pedestal. Go ahead. No need to be gentle.

3. Rear back, let the ball fly and wait for the fun at impact.

4. WHAP! Revenge at last! Feel the tension leaving your body.

5. Smile and head for work relaxed, refreshed and rejuvenated.

Eric commented: "There's even a snooze option so that you can get up more than once."

Dawn chorus: Seen in a department store in Tokyo: a Japanese clock designed on military principles.

Instead of an alarm, you hear a trumpet play *Reveille* and a little voice hollers: "Time to get up! Time to get up!"

Suddenly the American habit of keeping firearms at home for impulsive use seems eminently sensible.

BROKER AND BROKER STILL

Men in gay suits: There have been some interesting misunderstandings in Hong Kong among a certain breed of Men in Dark Suits, we hear.

The formal Cantonese phrase for fund manager is *gay gum ging lei*. But in street talk, they are *fun lo* or *gay lo* — the second of which also means homosexual.

Gwailo [foreigners] who are not absolutely confident about their Cantonese are recommended to use the full, formal term to avoid making potentially embarrassing contacts at cocktail parties:

"How nice to meet a *gay lo*. What? You're a fund manager? Leave my home at once! Honey, call the fumigators."

Your number's up: The Stock Exchange of Hong Kong has just released a fascinating bit of information. The number of official members of the exchange is 666.

We naturally thought of the *Book of Revelation* chapter

XIII, which tells of the rise of the Beast, sometimes called the Anti-Christ: *This calls for wisdom. If anyone has insight, let him calculate the number of the Beast, for it is man's number. His number is 666.*

The people of the Beast, who are identified with the number 666, have special trading powers, says the Bible. *No one could buy or sell unless he had the mark, which is the name of the Beast or the number of his name.*

Ominous, huh?

This revelation coincides with allegations by superstitious types that Mr Chim Pui-chung's recent bout of financial wrangles with the stock exchange were caused by negative mystical forces in the area of the Legislative Council where he sits. This is hard to believe, since he sits close to the Rev Fung Chi-wood, who must surely exude good vibrations.

Anyway, Lai See would like to make it clear that we are no way suggesting that the share market community is working for the Anti-Christ and the forces of darkness.

Not knowingly, anyway.

Expansionary dong: Now we will not tolerate any schoolboyish tittering while reading this item, so compose yourself.

Architect Charles Brown of Pollocks Path, the Peak, Hong Kong came across a shocking headline in the *Cambodia Times.*

"Bigger Dongs For Vietnamese" it said.

In fact, financial ministers in Hanoi have arranged for the printing of new, larger denomination dong banknotes.

It must be a nightmare being a headline-writer working on currency articles about the dong's ups and downs.

A newspaper in Asia printed a story about the dong and the US dollar with the headline "Dong dangles between 6½ and 7".

They can speak for themselves.

All a loan: Maurice Gardette, boss of the Cafe de Paris, wanted to refurbish his Hong Kong restaurant.

So he phoned Standard Chartered Bank and asked whether he could borrow HK$300,000.

Bank staff told him that they had a special arrangement for this kind of loan. "If you deposit HK$300,000, you can borrow 95 per cent of this sum," they told him.

If he already had the HK$300,000, surely he could lend it to himself?

We wonder if Standard Chartered has really thought this one through.

Market swells: Brassiere experts in Hong Kong have noticed an increase in the size of their target market. The standard bra size across Asia used to be 34-A but it has been replaced by 34 C.

Now don't scoff. This is important. Not only will it increase raw material costs, but the average bra is made up of 20 separate pieces of material, sewn together in a 23-stage operation. A swelling in the market dimensions means a great deal of adjustment for the manufacturers.

We are indebted to analyst Matthew Mo of South China Brokerage for this information, which he gleaned from an in-depth study of Topform International, Hong Kong's recently-listed bra-maker.

"It is believed that lingerie, especially brassieres, is the one area where working women with multiple roles can remind themselves that they are still women," he writes.

Just remember that the next time you are in a board meeting and you have completely forgotten what sex you are. Unbutton your shirt. If you are wearing a bra, you are either a woman or one of those strange creatures Ted Marr attracts to his Shanghai parties.

Mr Mo reckons the bra firm is a sure investment.

"Topform has adopted a two-pronged approach to growth," he writes.

Now there's a man unashamed to state the obvious.

Forex blues: Dana Sather of American Appraisal Hong Kong received an interesting fax from the forex people at L & D Investments.

It contained a chart with various interesting lines on it. A note at the bottom said: "Breaking through above blue line, you can continue to sell US$, under blue line you can continue to buy US$."

Dana said: "I think I should get a new fax line. I couldn't tell which of the lines was blue and which were other colours."

Taxing ideas: Beancounting firm Price Waterhouse is handing out notepads to journalists in the run-up to the Budget. To educate newshounds, each page has a thought-provoking maxim about finance on it.

The first on the list is interesting in the present democracy debate, and the last one has a real cynical Hong Kong flavour.

Taxation without representation is tyranny − James Otis, 1761.

Those who have some means think that the most important thing in the world is love. The poor know that it is money − Gerald Brenan, 1978.

We may see the small value God had for riches by the people he gives them to. − The Pope, 1727.

Money may not bring happiness, but at least you can be miserable in comfort − anon.

Old accountants never die, they just lose their balance – anon.

The love of money is the root of all evil – St Paul, 1st century.

Evil is the root of all money – anon.

But Price Waterhouse missed our favourite tax quotation. Bob Hope, talking about his wealthy former partner Bing Crosby, said: "Bing doesn't pay income tax any more. He just asks the government what they need."

Dislocated: Citibank in Hong Kong sent out letters to its customers in Repulse Bay. "Commencing January 26, 1993, our Repulse Bay Branch will be located to larger premises to serve you better," it said. "The new address is: Ground floor, Caroline Centre, Yun Ping Road, Causeway Bay, Hong Kong."

Several Repulse Bay residents, including John Tjia, were surprised by this. How can the bank serve them better by moving to the other side of the island?

We just hope Citibank Hong Kong does not do anything rash in a bid to serve customers even better still, by moving the entire operation to spacious offices in Burkino Faso.

Best analysis of a Hong Kong broker's statement: Dr Brian Brown of the Department of Diagnostic Sciences, Hong Kong Polytechnic tried to work out what was meant by a Hoare Govett Securities analyst quoted as saying:

"We might see some further index pull-back and we may see some see-saw movement but I think in the end it will either end up with some sideways movement or minor gains."

After much analysis, this can only mean:

It might go up a bit.

It might go down a bit.

It might go up a bit and down a bit.
It might stay about the same.

This brokerspeak is jolly clever stuff! No wonder those Hoare Govett boys always seem to get it right.

Are stocks high, or just brokers? Some Japanese brokers found a message in the Nikkei's record high, we heard from Makoto Nakamura of Daiwa Securities.

The Tokyo market hit a peak of 38,915.87 in 1989.

In Japanese, 398 is *sa ba ku,* meaning "a desert", 15 is *i ko,* meaning "to go", and 87 is *wa na,* "a trap".

This indicates that the market itself was sending investors a message: you are heading into a trap, and will be left in the wilderness.

It was right.

Financial prediction of the month, or possibly year, comes from technical analyst James Dines, in the *Asian Wall Street Journal:*

"The trend will continue until it ends."

Off screen: All hell broke loose on the stockmarkets on April 9, 1992.

Hong Kong business reporter Gareth Hewett phoned James Osborn at Exchange Square to pick up some local colour:

Hewett: Christ, mate, have you seen the markets?
Osborn: Yes, I saw them.
Hewett: Well, what's the view? What are your boys saying?
Osborn: "Switch off the screens."
Hewett: What?
Osborn: We're telling people to switch off their screens. Mine's off. I am not looking at it at these prices. If you do,

you tend to take it personally. You get a twitch in your right hand to make towards a calculator and see how much you've lost.

Hewett: Mmmmm.

Osborn: I am switching mine back on again on Monday to see how things are going. But if it's still bad, it's going straight off again.

Well, that gives you a taste of the atmosphere at Exchange square. You cannot describe brokers as wildly overconfident.

State of the art: Called Thornton Management late one afternoon. A taped message replied, giving a list of departments and direct lines for each of them.

Gosh, how wonderfully efficient, we thought.

We called each of these numbers, and got the same taped message on each one. Isn't technology wonderful?

Debt's life: Bella Dobie of NMD & D advertising got a stern letter from HongkongBank. It told her off for not being deeply enough in debt.

It said: "We note that the utilisation of your overdraft facility has been relatively low and would expect it to be used more actively with swings from debit to credit. If there is no improvement in the next review, we may consider to impose a commitment fee of ½ per cent per annum on the undrawn balance of your facility."

The "undrawn balance" is the bank's money that has NOT been borrowed. In other words, you pay them interest on money you haven't borrowed. This is brilliant.

Anyway, you heard what they said, Ms Dobie. Get spending. Become destitute and make your bank manager's day.

Guide to the new Japanese brokerspeak:
Medium Term Buy: A loss-maker.
Long Term Buy: A major loss-maker.
Speculative Buy: Horrible, but the finance director bought me a good lunch.
Short Term Buy: The stock is about to be ramped.
Strong Buy: The stock is now being ramped and is about to crash.
Hold: Sell.
Sell: Too late, you mug!

Canny Ken: Ken Madgwick of Repulse Bay went into a branch of HongkongBank and asked for a bag of HK$2 coins and a bag of HK$1 coins. He was told that the first bag would be free, but the second bag would attract a handling fee of HK$1.

"So I took my 'free' bag of coins, walked between the ropes to another teller, and was given another bag of coins, also free.

"I'm not sure if they're crazy, or it's me."

On the face of it: An analyst was complaining about the offer document details in Hong Kong tycoon Li Ka-shing's plan to buy Cavendish back from its shareholders.

"These is no valuation of cash holdings," he said. They don't have to provide one, but it would have been nice. Cash is pretty easy to value, you know, even if you want to do it quickly," he added.

Face value: Fax received from Dana Sather of American Appraisal Hong Kong:

"We read with interest about the analyst who was complaining about Li Ka-shing not providing a valuation of Cavendish's cash holdings.

"As a truly independent valuation firm, we would like to offer our services.

"In fact, for KS, I will do the valuation certificate myself, for free. He just has to let me know how much cash there is."

Doesn't sound difficult, this cash valuation business.

Out with it: Stick your cashpoint card into one of those fancy new multi-colour ATMs at the Bank of East Asia to get some money, and what happens?

You get a question: "Do You Wish To Have Advice?"

The odd thing is that whether you press "Yes" or "No", you never get any advice.

We expect it to laugh and say something like: "You shouldn't really be taking more money out, with YOUR income."

How to read the mind of a South Korean broker:
What he says: "The market is see-sawing."
What he thinks: *I'm completely lost.*
Says: "The rebound was due to technical factors."
Thinks: *God knows why it went up.*
Says: "We see a single-day reversal."
Thinks: *Oops, I've been telling everyone it will go up.*
Says: "It touched on a technical support."
Thinks: *Oops, I've been telling everyone it will go down.*
Says: "There was some sideways movement."
Thinks: *We took the day off because we were all drunk.*
Says: "Long distance call on line two. Gotta go."
Thinks: *Better get off this phone before I make a complete fool of myself.*

Why Hong Kong brokers can't stay in the black: There was a power cut at the Jockey, a popular Suits hang-out in Swire House.

In the sudden blackness, staff leapt to the entrance and bolted the doors, so drinkers could not make a speedy exit without paying their bills.

An annoyed broker rang Lai See to complain about this. "How do you know it was locked?"

"I tried to make a quick exit," he admitted.

We had almost exactly the same conversation with another broker who rang to complain about the same incident yesterday. He had also tried the doors.

There's a lesson here somewhere.

Strangest coincidence in the Hong Kong financial scene:

HongkongBank's big purchase in the United States is called Marine Midland.

HongkongBank's big purchase in the United Kingdom is called Midland.

What does "China" *(Jung-gwok* in Cantonese and *Chung-gwo* in Mandarin) mean?

The literal translation is "Mid-Land".

Have we stumbled upon some sort of massive global conspiracy?

Easiest questionnaire: Standard Chartered Bank sent out a leaflet to customers with a question on the front: "Do you know how to get the most from an ATM?"

Recipient Tony Giles of Lantau wrote back: "I would have thought a two-ton truck and an oxy-acetylene torch would do the trick."

Maxwell House: Brokers who keep swapping ghastly jokes about businessman Robert Maxwell may like to send them in a more fruitful direction.

Corgi Books' Eileen Dover is putting together a compilation of jokes called *A Drop in the Ocean.* All proceeds go to a fighting fund aimed at compensating the hapless unpensioned.

We hope it fares better than the feeble *Robert Maxwell Joke Book* that came from Blake Publishing in early May.

It sank without trace. Which is a darn sight more than can be said for etc, etc.

Unlucky Gym: Bankers, lawyers and doctors have taken to spending a couple of hours mid-day in the Gym, a posh fitness centre in Central.

Hard work? Nope. They nip into the relaxation room, a chamber with vibrating beds, and have a nap.

One chap, who we'll call Mr Complete-Banker, unwisely left the telephone number with his secretary.

First stroke of bad luck: a financial emergency broke out.

Second stroke of bad luck: his boss decided to make the call.

The boss phoned the number, and a staff member at the Gym paged Mr Complete-Banker and got no answer. She found him asleep in the relaxation room.

"I'm sorry, he's asleep," she told the boss. "If you'd like to leave a message, I'll give it to him when he wakes up."

The boss went berserk.

A colleague of Mr Complete-Banker ran to the Gym to wake up his friend.

Gym staff have now been briefed to give discreet, non-committal answers to similar calls.

Hidden agendas of Taiwanese share salesmen:

I have a useful tip for you: Please take this useless stock off my hands.

I have a speculative tip for you: Please take this disaster-to-be off my hands.

I have some inside information for you: I have a wild

rumour for you.

I have a wild rumour for you: I am making this up as I go along.

Sterling work: Scott Rosen of Hoare Govett Asia received an invitation to subscribe to a publication called *Currency Confidential.*

You can buy one year's subscription for US$595 or £399 (an exchange rate of US$1.49).

You can take out four months' subscription for US$193 or £99 (an exchange rate of US$1.95).

You can buy *Using Currency Options More Effectively* for US$99 or £60 (an exchange rate of US$1.65).

You can buy *Corporate Management of Foreign Exchange* for US$85 or £50 (an exchange rate of US$1.70).

"I think it may be useful for the editorial department to provide some copies of the report to the marketing department," said Scott.

Last cent: Computer consultant Julian Russell of Mid-Levels got a letter from HongkongBank.

"We write to advise you that, at the close of business on June 6, 1992, our records showed that withdrawals from your above-mentioned account had exceeded the available balance by HK$00.75," it said.

A telephone number is kindly provided in case Mr Russell needs advice on raising this sum.

The stamp on the letter was 80 cents.

"If they had paid my overdraft for me, they would have ended up five cents ahead," said Mr Russell.

On the job: The banking community in Hong Kong is abuzz with tales about the senior foreign banker in the territory who was caught having a romantic liaison with a lady in

Guangzhou.

The Public Security Bureau took a stern view of the case, and so did the banker's overseas bosses. They made him follow the rule of Chinese law, and go through a humiliating procedure of collecting signatures from local people to absolve him.

The unhappy gentleman has been recalled and is leaving Hong Kong with his tail between his legs, so to speak.

This sad tale should not be confused with another tale (hopefully apocryphal) about a Hong Kong stockbroker who had an improper assignation with a lady of the night in Shenzhen.

Just as he was leaving, she said: "Oh by the way, do you have any communicable sexual diseases, such as AIDS?"

"No," he replied.

"Good," she said. "I don't want to catch *that* again."

Not a good idea: Whoops. The Nigerian fraudsters have been aiming their enticing little scam in a new direction.

A source in China yesterday told us that fraudulent business letters have been received at a joint venture hotel in Xian. They are the usual invitations asking for details of the recipient's bank account.

"I'm thinking of opening up a Bank of China reminbi account for them," said the recipient. "See how far they get with that."

Suddenly we feel deeply sorry for the scamsters.

Most absent-minded party-goer: Guy Devenish, a fun-loving stockbroker at the Hong Kong offices of Smith New Court, had a pleasant evening at a rather riotous, Suitpacked New Year's Eve dinner party at Bentley's seafood restaurant in Prince's Building.

He and Brian Nicholl, a senior fund manager at Pierson's, then sauntered over to the Mandarin Oriental for a nightcap to celebrate the early hours of 1992.

However, Mr Devenish was getting just a little tired and emotional by this time. Mr Nicholl, who is a client of the stockbroker, decided to drive his friend home.

He sympathetically heaved the near-lifeless carcass into his shiny Honda saloon, and re-entered the hotel to find another body from his party to load into the vehicle.

Several minutes later, Guy Devenish awoke to find himself in a car in front of the Mandarin Oriental, with lots of drivers hooting behind him.

A few cells deep within his brain cortex (the only part functioning at the time) assumed that this was his own car, and so he drove home to Shiu Fai Terrace, parked it in the garage, and went to sleep.

At about 2 pm on New Year's Day, he received a call from Mr Nicholl.

"What happened to my car?" asked a worried Mr Nicholl, phoning from his home on the Peak.

"I don't know. *I* haven't got it," replied Mr Devenish.

Mr Nicholl said he was going to report the theft to the police.

The stockbroker dragged his weary bones down to the garage and peered in his parking space.

There it was.

A fellow stockbroker commented with a sigh: "If one must steal cars, one should really try not to steal them from one's clients."

Brother in arms: At the time of writing there has been a suspicious absence of armed raids on Hong Kong jewellery shops for some time.

Stock market activity has been sluggish as well.

"Well of course they're linked, you idiot," said a mild-mannered broker with whom we raised this issue yesterday.

"It is all to do with liquidity and the velocity of asset-movement in Hong Kong."

We say: are we locking up the right people?

Serious dosh: You are just leaving a swish cocktail party at the Island Shangri-La.

You check in your wallet to see if you have enough change for a taxi.

You discover you have not.

"Oh dear," you say as loudly as you can. "Does anyone have change for a billion-dollar banknote?"

Wow. A hush of reverent, worshipful awe descends on the room, and a glorious light shines.

This scenario was a very real fantasy for a group of would-be buyers, we learned from Jeremy Platts, soon-to-leave head of the Commercial Crime Bureau's intelligence section.

A salesman working in Hong Kong claimed to have a US$1 billion banknote, issued by the US treasury in 1875, and still legal tender — so he said.

A group of Australian investors were offered it for the bargain price of US$60 million. The Australians, who were in the sheep-farming business, fell for it, and flew to Hong Kong to clinch the deal.

Luckily, Hong Kong's Commercial Crimes Bureau got wind of it, reached the sheepfarmers first, and foiled the plan. The scamsters fled.

But the billion-dollar banknote later resurfaced in other parts of Asia, said Mr Platts. It could still be extant.

Lai See's tip: do not offer to change billion-dollar notes for anyone you don't know really really well.

It won't wash: Biochemist Danny Gohel, of the University of Hong Kong, showed us a letter received from a tourist who collects banknotes.

It was from Armin Veith, a German citizen, who met a Hong Kong traveller while in Egypt recently. The traveller handed over samples of our currency, including a Hong Kong $100 banknote.

This is what Mr Veith's letter says:

"From my journey I took banknotes back to Germany from every country some.

"At home I washed them with water and soap and ironed them to smooth them out. All of them became very nice.

"Only your 100 HK$ note lost its paint while I was iron it. It's not a good quality.

"Hong Kong – hi-tech and this bad quality of print? I think you have to talk with the Government because of this."

So much for Hong Kong's reputation as money-laundering capital of the world.

Cash call: The mobile phone of Hong Kong businessman Jeff Heselwood rang on a Saturday morning.

Heselwood: Hello. Jeff Heselwood.

Hong Kong Bank: Hello. This is Hong Kong Bank. We have received a cheque signed by you, drawn on Jeff Heselwood Communications Ltd and payable to Mr Jeff Heselwood. There is an alteration on the cheque. Should we pay?

Jeff told us afterwards: "Of course I said no. Let him wait for his money like everyone else."

Door bell: Concerned about why the Hong Kong stock market has been so unsettled recently?

Never fear. The cause has been located, using the latest scientific techniques. A patch of negative mystical force was discovered right by the front door of the stock exchange, next to the main escalators to Exchange Square One and Two.

The *fung shui* man who discovered it also knew how to put it right. Music must suddenly appear whenever anyone enters the stock exchange, he said.

They've now fixed it up. As soon as you stride through the door, a horrible tinny whine (you know, a monophonic computer-chip tone) plays one of a selection of Christmas carols.

Our presence triggered "Silent Night".

This was on a sweltering 32 degrees celcius morning in August. The device is to be left on permanently. We are not making this up.

We are not saying that the stock exchange bosses are unbelievably gullible, but somebody is definitely making a fool of somebody.

RUN! THE LAWYERS ARE REVOLTING

The following dialogue took place in a popular bar in a well-known and prestigious commercial complex in Central, Hong Kong. Its precise location CANNOT be revealed because of possible legal reapercus, er, repurcush, er, reparcush, er, okay, look, it took place in Brown's Wine Bar at Exchange Square.

The dialogue is a verbatim transcription, but personal names have been changed to avoid identification.

ME: Hello, Mr Expat-Lawyer. Heard the latest joke going round? Why is California full of lawyers and New Jersey full of toxic waste?

MR EXPAT-LAWYER: (Silence.)

ME: Because New Jersey got first choice. Ha ha ha!

MR EXPAT-LAWYER: (Leaves.)

I performed a quick breath-and-armpit test and eliminated two possible reasons why he had left. Then it clicked. He had not enjoyed the joke. This was my first inkling that perhaps some lawyers do not appreciate the craze of making lawyer jokes.

I was dumbfounded. Could it be that this cheery pastime, believed to have started in California, but now a popular bar-room activity all over the civilised world, is actually causing the more tender-skinned of our legal brethren and sistren to feel heartache?

Impossible. Lawyers don't have hearts, they have cash registers. Ha ha ha.

Sorry, couldn't resist that. Where were we? Oh yes, my deep and sincere remorse.

I discovered my friend, who we are calling Mr Expat-Lawyer (remember, this is not his real name), in a different bar two days later.

This time we talked about The Touchy Subject like grown men. He said he had been thinking of writing an essay on the subject, and had written some notes.

"It is about time the lawyers of the world stood up for themselves against this insidious campaign of image-poisoning being carried out against the profession. I am talking about the constant stream of lawyer jokes, lawyer cartoons and, on a more subtle level, the conversational jibes against the innocent but greatly maligned people who make their living by dispensing the law, that precious but thankfully ever-renewable resource.

"Esteemed colleagues, it is time to exorcise this image. Otherwise, if left to fester, it could eventually grow to a degree where the public preferred not to use our services. It could get to the point where lawyers are publicly abused."

Only days after this discussion, I came across a shocking item of news and realised that he was not joking. At least in Asia, no one has yet proposed an annual festival during which members of the public can commit acts of violence against members of the legal profession without fear of prosecution.

This cannot be said, however, of the United States. A senator by the name of David Thomas, Republican for Greenville, South Carolina, has proposed that the South Carolina legislature consider an "open season on lawyers". This would be on the same lines as duck-hunting season, grouse-shooting season and so on.

Mr Thomas actually introduced a Bill to permit it.

A similar Bill was drawn up in Texas.

A Bill to Regulate the Hunting and Harvesting of Lawyers

372.01. Any person with a valid rodent or armadillo hunting licence may hunt and harvest lawyers for recreation and sporting (non-commercial) purposes.

372.02. Taking of lawyers with traps or deadfalls is permitted. The use of currency as bait, is, however, prohibited.

372.03. The wilful killing of lawyers with a motor vehicle is prohibited, unless such vehicle is an ambulance being driven in reverse. If a lawyer is accidentally struck by a motor vehicle, the dead lawyer should be removed to the roadside and the vehicle should proceed to the nearest car wash.

372.04. It is unlawful to chase, herd, or harvest lawyers from a yacht, helicopter or aircraft.

372.05. It is unlawful to hunt lawyers within 100 yards of BMW, Porsche or Mercedes dealerships, except on Wednesday afternoons.

372.06. It is unlawful for a hunter to wear a disguise as an accident victim for the purpose of hunting attorneys.

When Mr Thomas was asked by members of the press what his purpose had been, he just said it was a joke.

A journalist on the *Charlotte Observer* wrote an editorial about this subject. He wrote: "It is terrible to joke about the killing of human beings.

"Or even of lawyers, for that matter."

Anyway, our sympathy for Hong Kong's overpriced lawyers was tempered somewhat after someone reported this exchange:

Victim: What are your fees?
Lawyer: It's HK$20,000 for three questions.
Victim: Wow. Isn't that a bit steep?
Lawyer: Yes. And what was your third question?

HUMAN WRITES

OTHER writers may call me a traitor, but it must be said: there is quite frankly TOO MUCH to read in this world today. Too many feature articles, too many magazines and books, too much printed matter of every kind.

I hasten to add that I am not referring to the volume you are holding in your hands.

Oh no, I mean those really obscure publications that fill shelf after shelf in libraries and newsstands. They bring confusion to the reader, and a damaging dissipation of money and energy to the publishing industry.

Did you know that there are now 74,000 scientific magazines published regularly in the world? Even the Institute of Scientific Information in America, one of the world's main bodies to keep track of scientific papers, only takes note of 4,500 or so.

So what happens to the other 69,500?

The grim truth is this. Probably nobody reads them. No

scientists. No librarians. Not even the MOTHERS of the writers. And since the magazines are not saved in libraries, probably no one will EVER read them.

This is devastating from a philosophical point of view.

Until now, words have always been written to be read. But the words of these writers are being written only for the sake of being written. They use up trees, time, money and will power.

Yet the only benefit they bring to the world is in terms of personal therapy for the writers. Could not the money be better spent on getting professional help for these people?

Now I don't want anyone to think that I am a killjoy, against the whole idea of specialist magazines. On the contrary.

Some of my favourite magazines are the tiny ones. Who could resist being charmed by *Maledicta*, a journal that has been going for more than decade, devoted entirely to the use of bad language in the world?

And what more suitable magazine could there be for these material times than *Acquisitions Monthly*, a UK publication popular with yuppies?

For the eclectic diner, there is no more vital publication on today's magazine racks than *Chile Pepper*, the Magazine of Spicy Foods. This is hot reading in every sense of the word, featuring titillating pin-ups of red chilli peppers.

A fascinating publication I came across recently was *Collector*, the trade journal read avidly by loan shar – er, debt collectors everywhere.

To digress for a moment, I wonder what happens to subscribers who get behind in their subscriptions? Do they send round the boys? Or do they rely on the professionalism of the subscribers, who should eventually turn themselves in?

Then of course there was the Hong Kong-based magazine *The Emigrant*, which announced that it will stop printing before the end of this year because of falling circulation, after a couple of successful years as a monthly magazine.

The most frustrating job in Asia must have been circulation manager for *The Emigrant*. One by one, all their most ardent readers left town.

Another magazine I would be doubtful about working on is *Good Dog!*, published in South Carolina, United States. This is a consumer magazine, reviewing products for dogs, such as dog food.

I mean, what are the mechanics of doing a food review on something that comes in a tin called Fido-Slobber-Chunks? Not a subject I like to think about too hard.

I imagine that the magazine *Money Laundering Alert*, published in Miami, would be very popular in places such as Hong Kong and Taiwan, where people like to keep up to date on that sort of thing.

There is a new magazine in the United States which focuses on recycling - a popular subject in this environmentally aware age. The editors have called it *Garbage*. Odd. I thought it was quite good, actually.

It seems as if every possible idea in the world has already been turned into a full scale magazine.

But this is not true. I hope readers realise that I am proposing this moratorium on new publications at considerable cost to myself, since like most writers, I have long harboured secret desires to be editor of my own magazine.

In order to demonstrate my sincerity, I hereby throw open to the world the launch plans for several magazines I had planned to start over the next few years, but will now forgo.

1. GADGET ADDICTION WEEKLY. Do you own three or more small metal items in black leather slipcases? Such as a personal hi-fi, a beeper, a mobile phone, a handheld video game or a digital diary? Are you thinking of

splashing out on a pocket television? If so, you are a gadget addict. But don't worry — find out you can live a normal life: only in *Gadget Addiction Weekly*.

2. OBSCURITY. Bored to tears with magazines full of celebrities? This is what you need: a stylish glossy magazine in full colour, featuring in-depth interviews with total nobodies. Non-entity status is guaranteed. Even an appearance in this magazine counts as minor celebrity status, so nobody is allowed to appear twice.

3. THE FILLED-IN PUZZLER. Want to impress your friends, colleagues, wife, children? This is a magazine full of complex cryptic crosswords, tough word squares and difficult general knowledge quizzes. But ALL the answers have been filled in for your convenience in realistic simulated handwriting. Just leave it lying around. When ordering, please specify style of writing (a) pencil (b) ballpoint pen, or (c) fountain pen. Also specify amount of crossings-out, working notes and corrections to be made: (a) 30 per cent (b) 10 per cent or (c) none. Comes in a plain brown wrapper.

And of course:

4. MAGAZINE LISTINGS MONTHLY: The most necessary publication of the decade! An A-Z of all the magazines to be printed this month, including special feature-length articles on new ones being launched. This month's special focus: *Magazine Listings Monthly*.

I think the above four magazines are as likely to be successful as any other magazine named in this article, but I will never launch them myself.

I will stick to my crusade, telling the world that there are too many publications on this planet.

But can anyone tell me the best way of getting this message across? The only way I can think of is to start a journal. Anyone know a good publisher?

THE CAT WHO LEARNED THE FAX OF LIFE

Dan Peterson of the Hong Kong Channel, the hotel in-house television service, was fast asleep at his tranquil flat in Yung Shue Wan, Lamma island.

Images of his home facsimile machine kept intruding into his dreams, which seemed a curious thing to happen. As dawn broke, he half awoke — and heard the unmistakable sound of the fax clicking and whirring.

Since it was early on a Sunday morning, he decided not to get up. "I'll read it later," he thought to himself.

Then he realised something with a start. That was NOT the sound of his fax receiving a document. It was the noise it made when it *sent* one.

Intruders are not uncommon in Lamma. But why should one break into his house to send faxes from his machine?

He leapt out of bed and caught the guilty party red-handed: Spangle, his chubby 10-year-old black and white cat.

Spangle had been warming his stomach on the machine

and purring in time with the buzzing it made — then he had started playing with the buttons: Dan found error messages on the machine from seven locations, including one in Singapore and two in North America.

"I had to pay for them, too," said Dan.

Spangle was probably trying to fax Oliver's delicatessen for a delivery of smoked salmon.

● Following yesterday's item about Spangle the faxing cat, requests have arrived signed by other cats who wanted to know how you do it, since most fax machines won't function without a sheet of paper being placed in the tray.

Spangle tells us that the simplest way is to watch your master when he inputs numbers into the stored memory — especially machines with one-touch dialling.

You then climb onto the machine and press all the buttons with long-distance numbers.

Even if there is no paper in the tray to be transmitted, the machine will still attempt to make a connection, and your master will get a series of small but infuriating long-distance bills, like Spangle's master.

If it is a G3 fax talking to a G2 fax it can take a long time, running up a big bill. If you find a multiple dialling button, you can bankrupt your master. That'll teach him to economise on the gourmet cat food!

● Meanwhile, what we want to know is: has Hong Kong Telephone looked into this burgeoning new market?

They could call it PetFax, or MoggyMessage, or perhaps DogMess for short.

We could soon all be hearing from our domestic fauna.

Imagine coming into your office and your secretary says: "There's a DogMess on your desk."

SEX, OR, YOU FLIPPED TO THIS CHAPTER FIRST, DIDN'T YOU?

SEX is a word I have always wanted to start a feature article with. It is so dramatic, so attention-grabbing.

Oh look, I seem to have done it. How nice.

I have one friend who will greatly approve of this, on philosophical grounds: an advertising man known to his friends as Tosh.

This creative gentleman is a great believer in the power of primal instincts.

Of course, in the advertising industry it has long been held that you can sell anything with sex. But mention this and people usually think of those stupid promotional posters or calendars, in which you get girls in bikinis grinning and holding flanges and widgets.

Ninety-nine per cent of that is low-brow junk of the most crass sort. No, sex should be used in an intelligent, humorous way, says Tosh.

An early advertisement of his showed a chap looking at

something on a beach through a pair of binoculars. The slogan was: "What a great pair of floppies." It was an ad for a computer.

He was later making a pitch for a campaign to sell denture glue: can you think of any product less sexy?

Tosh made a storyboard for a television ad in which a James Bond type is kissing lots of women. He turns to the camera and taps his dentures. "Their bones turn to jelly. My teeth stay rigid," says Bond.

The adman faced a major challenge when he was pitching for an account to sell disposable contact lenses. How can one make that appeal to the baser instincts?

The visual part was a close-up photograph of a woman wearing glasses and looking seriously concerned.

The copy read:

"Spectacle-wearers!

"So what if your partner looks attractive when smartly groomed during the day?

"The truth is: you can't even SEE him at night with your specs off, can you?

"You just curl up with an indistinguishable blur, right?

"Face facts. IT MIGHT NOT EVEN BE YOUR SPOUSE.

"Get Kleer-View All-Nite Disposable Contact Lenses, and discover who you are sleeping with.

"Think about it before you get in bed tonight.

"THAT MAY NOT BE YOUR PARTNER IN THERE."

His boss agreed that Tosh was genuinely offbeat and off-the-wall. And also off his head. This unappreciative employer, a philistine to the very top of his toupee, decided that his cheeky employee needed to be taught a lesson.

So he banished him to the account group that all creative types dread: The Public Service Announcements Section. I mean it is tough to give a public service announcement and degree of interest whatsoever. But make it alluring? Impossible, surely.

But you can't keep a good man down. Here is Tosh's rather startling, and I think worthwhile effort for the Blood Donation Service.

A photograph shows two clean-looking healthy young people looking longingly at each other over a candlelit dinner. Each is wearing a blood donors' badge.

The copy reads:

"They're sexy.

"And they're safe.

"They are the most desirable people of the 1990s.

"They are BLOOD DONORS.

"Every time they give blood, the contents of their veins are checked for HIV, the virus that carries AIDS.

"These two have given blood. They have also clearly discovered that they can go ahead and make their dreams come true. Tonight.

"Why don't you do the same?

"After that romantic meal, don't spoil the atmosphere by asking your partner to list everyone they have slept with for the past seven years.

"Just whisper: 'I give. Do you?'

"And hear her reply: 'I do.'"

So Tosh's copywriting style is not the most delicate in the world, but his conviction is strong. His day will come. It is a pity he is based in Asia, where prudery is rife.

It must be said, however, that sex is not attention-grabbing to everyone. This is a true story: at college, I did a thesis on gender-differences in vocabulary. I called it SEX AND PHILOLOGY. The sub-title was The Most Interesting Thing in the World and the Most Boring.

My tutor glanced at the two titles and then looked at me

over his *de rigueur* half-moon glasses. "But which is which?" he asked, with complete seriousness.

Some people are beyond salvation.

COMMERCIAL BREAK

Neutral stance: A recruitment advertisement in the *Hong Kong Standard* said:
 *A fashion co located in Kowloon Bay
 Seeks Asst Merchandiser
 Neither sex."*
Gay lib has finally reached Hong Kong.

Total CAD: A firm in Fenwick Street, Wan Chai, Hong Kong, advertised in the South China Morning Post for an assistant architect.
 "CAD is preferred but not essential," it said.
 Well, it's a good thing somebody wants to employ these sexist bounders.

Broadest product range: In an advertisement in *AmCham* magazine, the Hunan Cereals, Oils and Foodstuffs Import and Export Corporation of China tells readers that it offers:

"Fresh eggs, preserved eggs and other kinds of eggs". What other sort of eggs are there, other than bad eggs?

Bravest property marketing statement: There is a tempting offer in the LandPower Office Price Index for Hong Kong.
FOR SALE
Central
Shun Tak Centre
1,350, 1,400, 2,500 sq ft
High Floor
Full Obstructed Seaview

How courageous of them to market it this way. They did not let the fact that the sea view was fully obstructed dampen their marketing zeal.

Anyone want to buy Lai See's flat? Full sea view, completely obstructed by only six consecutive layers of buildings.

Self-starter: A boat-owner offered a 41-ft split-level sailing vessel for sale in the classified ad pages of the *SCMP*.

It says this boat comes with an "Onan generator". What is this? Some sort of rude magazine?

Quintessential: Reader Anita Lau was surprised by a recruitment ad in the *South China Morning Post* placed by an import-export firm in Kwun Tong:
Marketing Assistant.
Form 5. 1-2 years experience is essential but not necessary.

This must be designed to put off people who take what they read too literally.

Least enticing slogan for a food item: was the one we saw for Teenage Mutant Ninja Turtle Pudding Pies.

Fresh from the Sewer to You.

Venda vendor: This was spotted by Hong Kong-based Dave Cooper in an African publication:
Do You Want Some Portraits?
Framed portraits galore at the cheapest price!
For only 15 rand [about US$5] you may purchase the following framed portraits.
- *The Late President of Venda.*
- *The Former State President of Venda.*
- *Former Government Ministers of Venda.*
- *Former Deputy Ministers of Venda.*

You are at liberty to buy as many as you can afford.
Me first! Me first!

Jammy buggers: The new and rarely used Eastern Harbour Tunnel in Hong Kong had its first full-scale rush hour traffic jam one morning in March, 1991.

This was because there had been an accident, and police halted traffic in the tunnel for more than 15 minutes.

To pass the time, staff of the New Hong Kong Tunnel Co handed all drivers a flier which said: "Why Suffer The Congestion? Try The Eastern Harbour Tunnel."

Not Bad: News of what appeared to be the best-named magazine ever arrived in the form of a letter on our desk:

"We are updating our mailing list for our SIN NEWS publication.

"If we do not receive any reply, we would assume that you do not wish to continue receiving the SIN NEWS publication."

Breathlessly, we filled in the form — only to realise that SIN NEWS is short for *Singapore Investment News.*

Suddenly all prospects of illicit excitement vanish. Utterly.

Pillow talk: Have you seen the Eunos, the flashy new upscale car from Inchcape Pacific's Fidelity Motors? This remarkable vehicle has one of those cushions that come out of the steering wheel in case of a crash.

The ad says: "A Driver Side Airbag is standard. It's solid as a rock with the extra cabin rigidity of single piece outer body construction, reinforced pillars and door impact bars."

Sounds a bit hard for a cushion, doesn't it?

Back peddler: Duncan McInnes of the Official Receivers' Office in Queensway, Hong Kong, was peering in bafflement at an advertisement in the *South China Morning Post.*

An employer was seeking several "Female Ass Merchandisers" with two years experience.

Cheeky.

Tempus fugit: Irvan, the Hong Kong shop that sells vintage watches in the Central Building and at Seibu, has long had a tradition of witty advertising. But we are not convinced that their latest slogan is ideal for a timepiece specialist:

"Our watches go fast."

More truth in advertising: Alan Thompson of Ngo Kee-Fletcher noted that a Dragonair advertisement in *Dollersaver* says: "Phuket has been labelled 'Peral of the Andaman Sea'."

Having visited Phuket recently, Mr Thompson can confirm that the sentiment is accurate, although they have spelt "peril" incorrectly.

Penney wise: The Hong Kong office of J.C. Penney, the huge American retailer, is looking for a market representative, we hear from Darcy Roehling of American Express.

"Must have at least four years' experience in wearing apparels," says the advertisement.

Does it take four years for nudists to get their habit completely out of their system?

Short-sighted: Recruitment firm Drake Executive is seeking a deputy general manager for a Hong Kong garment firm.

"Reporting to the general manager, you will be responsible for overlooking the entire operation," says the ad.

Doesn't sound much of a challenge, does it? We could do that with our eyes closed.

Most self-explanatory item: One of the slogans of Union Rich Plastic Factory of Fo Tan, Hong Kong, is "Sysmbols Of Quality Products".

Most honest job description: Did you see that ad in the classifieds in which a firm in Wan Chai, Hong Kong was willing to pay someone to be a "B.S. Co-Ordinator"?

"At least three years of experience in main contractor's B.S. team is preferable," it said.

How amazing. We know several people who have been giving out B.S. free of charge for years, not realising that one could make a living as a B.S. Co-Ordinator.

By the way, shouldn't the proper title be "Bull Shit *Artist*"?

Humblest job ad: John Bosworth of Hong Kong organisation Project Chambers was surprised to see an advertisement in a Nepali newspaper recently. It said:

Wanted: One Peon for reputed travel agency. Salary as per experience and qualification. Please apply with full biodata and contact within a week. Post Box 3634 Kathmandu.

This didn't surprise Lai See, who has worked in various south Asian countries. In that region, the word "peon" is a recognised job description.

A typical peon's job application letter:
Dear Sir,
After being in employment for three years as a Serf, I was promoted to Underling two years ago. I believe I now have the requisite qualities to face the challenge of being a Peon.

Least suitable slogan: The television is bombarding Hong Kong with advertisements saying that Chevalier Telepoint phones are "in all the right places".
What clever ads. Pity that one place the most popular Chevalier Telepoint phone is not available is Chevalier shops.
They are due to arrive in three weeks.

Most far-fetched holiday ad: Holders of American Express cards in Hong Kong received a wonderful offer: "Try Brunei's rich culture, rampant jungles and exciting nightlife for a great four-day three-night break." Your HK$5,590 fee includes a free welcome drink, it says.
This cannot be the same Brunei we know. The one where alcohol is banned, even in hotels? Where women are hidden behind Muslim head dresses? Where nightclubs are unheard of?
"When I lived in Brunei I invited a friend to stay," a Hong Kong government man told us. "He took a quick look round and said: 'Lotta nuns round here, aren't there?'."

The worst-targeted campaign in the history of Asian advertising: On every skyscraper in Indonesia, through much of 1990 and 1991, there were huge, expensive signs, sometimes neon-lit, with the message "VISIT INDONESIA".
Ninety-nine per cent of the people who saw these signs already live in Indonesia.
The other one per cent were visitors who had already complied.

Cheekiest junk mail: Angela Barron of Stanley, Hong Kong, wife of BBC Asia correspondent Brian Barron, received a letter from cosmetics firm Erno Laszlo.

"A Range Of Skin Care Products Has Been Meticulously Selected To Induce Your Buying Whimp," it says.

How cruel and unfair. Mr Barron, a tough reporter who frequently reports from the midst of wars and riots, is not in the least bit wimpish.

Most enticing job: The Pacific Club Kowloon is inviting applications for someone to run the women's spa.

A "hands-on person" is required, says the ad.

Stop right there. We'll take the job. How much do we have to pay a month?

In the mood: Are you in the garment business? Do you want a manufacturer in China to make naughty items of underwear for you?

A businessman calling from Beijing told us such people should try Lude International Garments Co, which has opened in that fair city.

Just think of the slogans you could have:
When you feel rude, dress Lude.
Don't be nude, dude, go Lude.
Etc, etc.

Non-rechargable: Rex Baggaley of Hong Kong-based Waterford Wedgewood Pan Asia was on holiday in Africa recently.

Browsing in the *The Nation* newspaper of Kenya, he noticed an obituary. This said that the boss of Kenya Batteries had "expired".

Obviously a carefully chosen word.

Here today, gun tomorrow: Worried about the flood of guns pouring into Hong Kong? So are we.

What on earth can the Government do to stem the flow?

Oh well, the authorities must be pretty busy, what with all the tenders and contracts they are handling at the moment. The Government has just let it be known that it is seeking a person or persons to buy a supply of "used Smith and Wesson Revolvers".

Applicants should apply to the Government Supplies Department in Oil Street, Fortress Hill and mention reference PT/58/92.

Also on the authorities' shopping list: criminal types.

The same day, it was announced that a contract is available for the "Provision of Persons for Identification Parades". Just mention reference PT/50/92.

To win this lucrative contract, you have to assure the procurement division that you have an endless supply of shifty-looking people who appear capable of all manner of mischief.

We suggest that Heinz Grabner, manager of the Hong Kong Foreign Correspondents' Club, put in a bid for this one.

There's no way he could lose.

Flushed with success: Received a cutting from a hi-tech publication about Clean Living, the Hong Kong chain of laundry shops.

It said: "Clean Living, with 26 branches, has a main lavatory in Hunghom where all their laundry is washed every day."

Doesn't sound very hi-tech to us.

Bottom of the class: Have you seen the ads that have gone up in MTR stations all over town, advertising a function with a "babies" theme at Cityplaza this weekend?

At the top of the panel is a naked baby's bottom.

In the rest of the frame are various items, including *Parents* magazine and *Ours* magazine. Because of the layout, all these items appear to have fallen out of the bottom.

Now you don't need a doctorate in post-Freudian psychology

to deduce what the ad designer thought this particular job was a load of.

Bound for fame: A new public relations firm has jumped into the spotlight in Hong Kong. It is called Leapy Publicity Consultant. Leapy is sending letters to businesses:

Dear Boss,
Do you unsatisfy the market share of your products? . . .
Leapy can help you solve the above problem and let your products up to the top in the market. Please do not hesitate to mail on Morrison Hill Road Post Office 57237 Mr Leapy Leung for more detail.

Many advertisers we know would give their eye-teeth to do a campaign for this company. Example: "Got a big deal coming up? Feeling jumpy? Let Leapy hop to it."

Truth at all cost: Judith Cabot of Mid-Levels passed a clothes shop in Cameron Road, Kowloon, with a sign saying "HK$20. Silk Scarves."

The shopkeeper had printed above the sign "NO BARGAIN".

An admirable example of truth in advertising.

Dying to know: A public relations man we know, who shall go unnamed, decided he needed to let off steam. (Being nice all the time is depressing, oddly enough.)

So he has started a nasty newsletter called *The Word is DOG.*

The first issue includes a write-up of a new book about Princess Diana, to be launched by DOG.

"Based on a seconds-long sighting of the Princess during her visit here a few years back, the new book reveals:

• HOW Diana attempted to end it all in the back of the limousine by slashing her wrists with a banana.

• HOW she attempted to infuriate Charles by smiling out of the window at Charles' future Hong Kong subjects.

● HOW she publicly coughed into a tissue and set tongues wagging about a possible cold coming on.

● HOW her furtive glances at the car's fuel gauge masked the hideous pain of her broken heart.

"AND the secret wave she invented to signal to those in the know that Charles was a complete wally, was wearing socks that did not match his suit, and had smelly breath."

The book is called: *How 3.5 seconds With Diana Changed My Bank Account.*

Believe us: this spoof is no less believable and is probably better researched than Andrew Morton's best seller.

Ow wow: Received a press release from the Shanghai JC Mandarin hotel, saying that a chap called Michael Ow has been named general manager.

"Being one of the most outstanding minds amongst the hoteliers today, he is the leader to the fellow Singaporeans in Shanghai, the mentor to the local counterparts and a popular grassroots leader to the Chinese community," gushes PR girl Ong Meng Yoke.

Further excerpts: "Mr Ow is a man of wisdom, determination and dedication. He is intellectual, enthusiastic, positive and pragmatic .. Mr Ow is effectively bilingual in English and Mandarin. His great success in China is certainly not by chance, but a result of his unflagging energy, his drive to move on and his clear vision of life."

Not exactly a "warts-and-all" portrait, is it?

Unrequited: There is a rather sad advertisement on the noticeboard at the Wellcome supermarket in Perkins Road, Jardine's Lookout, Hong Kong.

For Sale:
One white wooden loveseat.
Hardly used.
What an admission to make in a public place.

AT LAST: A CURE FOR LOVE

CALL me a cynic if you like, but this is how I believe Cupid the Angel of Love goes about his business. The chubby archer and his henchmen/researchers sit around a big conference table every Friday afternoon on a cloud somewhere. Piled in the middle are charts, family trees, and telephone books for every country in the world, and, for all I know, one of those new-fangled computer disk data storage systems. They beaver away in excited, breathless silence, and every few minutes, one of the busy little imps will let out a squeal: "Yo! Got one."

What they are looking for are Perfect Mismatches: people in situations in which they have the potential to fall in love with PRECISELY the least suitable person.

The victim (the "lover") and the target (the "lovee") may be disastrously ill-paired for any of a number of reasons. The lovee may be the least convenient age, size, cultural background, marital status, religion, geographical situation, or sex. The lover may be a tone-deaf karaoke hobbyist with 15 cats, while the lovee may be a musical purist with a severe fur allergy.

Oh? You think I'm cynical? You think that only a thoroughly jaundiced observer would reckon most people fall in love with unattainable partners?

I have reached that conclusion after years of observation. In 1976, a social group of which I was part included an abnormally attractive young lady and an unusually beautiful young man. Just as the long summer vacation started, Miss Right and Mr Right fell irredeemably in love.

She fell in love with him. He fell in love with her older sister — a shy, homely girl with a severe speech impediment. I'm not making this up. There followed the most awkward summer I can remember. Cupid and his gang of sadists must have fallen off their clouds laughing.

But anyway, let's be positive about all this. There is no use crying over spilt single-rose vases. Love-sick brothers and sisters: we must FIGHT BACK against the wiles of the mischief-making Angel of Love.

In almost every culture around the world, there are remedies and potions designed to help the lover win the love of the lovee. A little research has convinced me that the best bet is to embark upon a game plan on the following lines.

1. Get a coffee grinder. You need two hairs from your body — one long and fine, one short and curly. The hairs should be ground very fine and mixed with coffee.

2. Fill your fridge with chocolate. The chemicals in chocolate bring out an emotional response in people who eat it. You want the victim, oops, I mean the lovee, to feel as emotional as possible.

3. There are various age-old tricks involving sugar cubes, which you should ask your grandmother about. The one of which I have heard involves writing your name and the

name of the lovee on sugar cubes and dissolving them in a mixture of rose water and honey. Check your local variations.

4. Check the weather forecast. Plan your attack for the first days of sunshine after a period of dull weather. The sudden increase in sunshine causes an increase in Vitamin D in the body, and thus causes the romantic "flutter" that young people feel in springtime. Second, the increase in periods of bright light causes a psychological mood change — the lovee is likely to be literally in a sunny mood for your attack.

5. Before you set off to get the lovee, have a shower to get rid of any stale sweat. And then do a workout WITHOUT having a shower afterwards. Don't put on any perfume — fresh perspiration contains super-powerful pheremones which are irresistible.

6. On the way out, deliver a photograph of the lovee to your local medium. There are various things he or she can do it. One method is to put the photo face down and burn candles on the back for three hours, and then turn it face up and burn candles on the front for three hours.

7. Before you reach this stage, you will have to have done some detective work and found out the lovee's movements. Psychologists reckon that chance meetings are always perceived as more romantic than planned ones. Meet the lovee "by chance" on a sunny afternoon, and ask them back to your place for a tea-break.

8. While the lovee is talking to you, drinking the "special blend" coffee (containing the body hairs), eating the chocolate, and being unconsciously affected by your pheremones, keep calling him/her by his/her name. Psychologists say that repeated use of a person's name make them feel closer to you. Don't say: "So what's up?" Say: "So, Melchizadek/Ethelina, what's up?"

9. During the evening, find an excuse to deliver a good photograph of yourself into the hands of the lovee. If he/she has a beautiful image of you on the mantelpiece day after day, the lovee is liable to forget that in real life your face spends most of its time displaying shifting patterns of acne.

10. Retain something belonging to the lovee when he or she leaves. All the old spells on this subject say you are recommended to take a garment worn next to the skin, but this may be hard to come by ("Goodness, I'm fresh out of undergarments. Would you mind leaving some of yours behind?"). If you do get a garment or some other object, this should then be buried under your doorstep. Some of the old recipes call for you to take body hair or skin scrapings from the lovee, but again, those are pretty hard to come by before you really know someone well. ("What was your name again? Do you mind if I take a skin scraping from your heel?")

11. The Beatles were wrong. Money can buy you love. It costs 1,000 yen. It comes in the form of a compact disc which you give to the lovee. When they play it, they feel an amazing compulsion to adore you. The songs are overlaid with a subliminal message. A voice repeats the phrase "Please love me" 5,000 times at frequencies so high that the listener is not conscious of hearing it. DO NOT PLAY IT WITH DOGS IN THE ROOM.

Some may complain about the hygiene level of some of these old methods, but love has never been a particularly hygienic pastime.

At the very least, doing something about your situation will take your mind off one of the hard truths of life: the chances are, he or she probably doesn't even know you are alive, and may remain in that blissful state whatever you do.

So be warned. Cupid has a way of winning these things.

Love is all around: You know all these Life Dynamics-type training organisations which have sprung up in Hong Kong? Well, a certain woman of our acquaintance from a chamber of commerce has sent us this idea for a series of courses called Seminars For Men Only. Apparently this list is doing the rounds of offices in the territory, with women faxing copies to each other.

She hopes one of Hong Kong's personal development firms will put them into practice, since there are a potential 2,968,252 candidates in the territory.

Men are warned: they may find the following list of training courses deeply offensive.

1. *Combatting Stupidity*
2. *You Too Can Do Housework*
3. *PMT: Learning When to Keep Your Mouth Shut*
4. *How to Fill an Ice Tray*
5. *We Do Not Want Sleazy Underthings For Christmas; Give Us Money*
6. *Parenting: No, It Does Not End With Conception*
7. *You: The Weaker Sex*
8. *Reasons to Give Flowers*
9. *How to go Shopping With Your Mate and Not Get Lost*
10. *The Remote Control: Reducing Your Dependency*
11. *Romanticism: Other Alternatives to Sex*
12. *How Not to Act Younger Than Your Children*

Are we jumping to conclusions, or do we detect the merest *soupcon* of disenchantment with our wonderful, dynamic sex?

Off-Peak: A woman from the Peak sent us the following ideas to add to the seminars for men series.

"In the interests of what little harmony exists in our household, I request that you do not use my name," she said. Her husband may be able to spot himself from her suggestions:

1. *How to Choose Your Own Shirt in the Morning.*
2. *You Too Can Cook a Meal.*
3. *How to Avoid Talking for Years About the Only Meal You Ever Cooked.*
4. *Control Buttons on the Washing Machine: Using Them in an Emergency, Such as When Your Wife and Maid are Away at the Same Time.*

Come on chaps. They are walking all over us with this one.

Hunted species: Large numbers of gentlemen — well, men, anyway — have rushed to the defence of their sex.

An introductory financial talk will be handled by Stuart McLintock of Wan Chai, whose chosen title is:

Credit Cards and Bottomless Purses: There IS a difference.

A motoring seminar will be handled by Godric Peters of Sha Tin, offering:

1. *Reversing a Car into a Parking Space Without Losing the No Claims Bonus.*
2. *Why Not to Top up Car Batteries with Perrier.*

The chaps from Noble House Ltd, Alan, Matt and Rich, offer some psychological training courses to get women in the right frame of mind:

1. *Accepting a Passive Role During Football Season.*
2. *Curbing the 'Toilet Seat is Up' Anger.*
3. *Cockroach-Killing Without Hysteria.*

The foundation course was drawn up by a shy but well-known international banker in Hong Kong, and is made up of five seminars:

1. *How to Get Dressed in Under Three Hours.*
2. *Yes, an Outfit Can be Worn More than Once.*

3. *Time: You can Relate to it in a Meaningful Manner.*
4. *Ultimate love: Leaving his Personal Drawers Alone.*
5. *Driving: Random Gear Selection.*

We chided the banker for remaining in the "name-and-address-supplied" category. "I am about to get married," he said, and then gave a deep sigh. "What it is to live in fear."

Seminal advice: Kevin Ward of Binnie Consultants found these seminars for women on a bulletin board:

1. *"Are You Ready to Leave?" – Definition of the Word 'Yes'*
2. *Appropriate Rhetorical Questions (formerly: "Honey, Do I Look Fat?")*
3. *Crying and Law Enforcement*
4. *Advanced Computing Seminar – Program Your VCR*
5. *Gaining Five Pounds vs. The End of the World – a Study in Perspectives*
6. *Driving: Approximating a Constant Speed*
7. *Sports Finals: Not a Game, a Sacrement*
8. *How to Earn Your Own Money*
9. *Telephone Translations: "Yeah Me Too" Equals "I Love You"*
10. *Beyond "Clean" and "Dirty": The Nuances of Wearable Laundry*

Base Elements: This "hazardous materials" guide to women (origin unknown) quickly became a classic of the fax humour circuit. But Lai See readers responded with a guide to men which was much sharper and harder hitting, which we have printed afterwards:

A GUIDE TO HAZARDOUS MATERIALS
   ELEMENT: *Woman.*
   SYMBOL: WO^2

ATOMIC MASS: *Accepted as 118 lbs but known to vary from 100-500lbs.*

FOUND: *Copious quantities in all areas.*

PHYSICAL PROPERTIES:

1. *Melts if given special treatment.*
2. *Bitter if incorrectly treated.*

CHEMICAL PROPERTIES:

1. *Has a great affinity for gold, silver, platinum and precious stones.*
2. *Activity greatly increases after alcohol saturation.*

COMMON USES:

1. *Highly ornamental, especially in sports car.*

TESTS:

1. *Pure specimen turns rosy pink when discovered in the natural state.*
2. *Turns green when placed beside a better specimen.*

HAZARDS:

1. *Highly dangerous except in experienced hands.*
2. *Illegal to possess more than one.*

A GUIDE TO HAZARDOUS MATERIALS

ELEMENT: *Man.*

SYMBOL: EG^0

ATOMIC MASS: *Most think they are 150 lbs but actually vary from 98 lbs to 650 lbs.*

FOUND: *In large quantities around alcohol outlets.*

PHYSICAL PROPERTIES:

1. *Made of much denser material than WO^2, especially between the ears.*
2. *Black lump in centre-left of chest is the hardest material yet discovered.*

CHEMICAL PROPERTIES:

1. *Turns a bright shade of crimson when asked to describe feelings.*

2. *Froths violently when placed in view of sports events.*

COMMON USES:

1. *Useful for unskilled labour, such as changing light bulbs, plugs.*
2. *Used as bed warmer by WO^2.*

TESTS:

1. *Becomes completely inert when faced with domestic chores.*
2. *Dissolves into tears (H^2O) when their team loses.*
3. *When placed near WO^2 in a bikini, middle portion of EG^0 is sucked in and upper portion thrust out.*

HAZARDS:

1. *Stupid.*
2. *Doesn't know it.*

FOREIGN EXCHANGE

THE foreign shopper leans over the counter and points to the miniature television-and-video combination. "Excuse me. How much is that in seashells?"

The shop assistant stabs the keys of her calculator. "At today's rates, it would be 84 large fluted cowrie shells, plus 3.5 small ones. You can pay the .5 in sand if you like."

"Do you accept dray-horses?"

A chart is consulted. "We no longer take any equine credit, I'm afraid, because they poo all over the axminster."

Is this the future of shopping?

Barter is definitely making a comeback in Asia. It ranges from cementing a transaction with a carton of Marlboro, all the way up to a recent airline deal between Vietnamese and Australian businessmen, in which the currency was seafood.

Barter has advantages, especially for travellers. Your Humble Narrator can proudly boast, with a reasonable degree of certitude, of having been conned by some of the most expert money-changing tricksters around the world.

It is not going to get any easier. Now all these small, once-cut-off nations (Slobnia and what's that other place? Hertzcar-Rentia?) are emerging into the international scene, that there are dozens more currencies for me to get confused over.

Here are some of the currencies the modern traveller has to cope with, with their values in US dollars at July 1990.

Already, nomads are starting to become familiar with the zlotys of Poland (about 9,300 to the US dollar), the lek of Albania (5.8 to the US dollar) and the Venuzuelan bolivar (48.3 to the US dollar).

Soon, dear reader, we will have to come to terms with the nguitrum of Bhutan (17 to the US dollar), the colon (that's right, as in intestine) of El Salvador (6.3), the quetzal of Guatamala (3.9), the tugrik of Mongolia (3.4), the dirham of Morrocco (8.6) , the metical of Mozambique (939), the lilangeni of Swaziland (2.64) and the Western Samoan taia (2.34).

Incidentally, if barter becomes popular in El Salvador, you had better be careful who you offer your colon to.

In this region, the Vietnamese dong is probably the most confusing, simply because the units are so tiny. On my first trip to Vietnam, I planned to head out of Ho Chi Minh City, so I decided to change a couple of United States notes. I decided to assume that any international banks I came across in the jungles of the Mekong Delta would lack 24-hour automatic teller machines.

I blithely presented my US$200 to the moneychanger, and he started to construct a replica of the Great Wall of China with wads of banknotes.

The value of one dong in US dollars fluctuates, but it tends to stay around its base rate of one dong = one speck of dirt.

There are one and two dong notes available in Vietnam, but most foreigners ignore them. There is not a great deal you can buy in tourist hotels for one-fiftieth of a US cent, even after group discount.

The local populace too prefer to deal in larger denominations. Women selling baguettes in the market had handfuls of 20 dong notes (two-fifths of a US cent) and 50 dong notes (one US cent).

As the moneychanger began to disappear from view behind the banknotes, I said: "Ahem. Don't you think it would be a better idea if you gave me the money in the largest denominations?"

"These ARE the largest denominations — 2,000 dong and 5,000 dong," he said.

My US$200 had become one million dong.

"Just round it off to the nearest 10 dong. I don't want to be too finicky," I said as a joke.

He didn't laugh.

I stuffed the money into a pouch, pushed it down the front of my trousers for safety, and then waddled out of the bank like the Michelin Man.

The first Westerner I met pointed to this immense lump in the front of my trousers and said: "What's that?"

"My dong," I replied.

My companion was less fortunate. He had only one of those money belts that looks like an ordinary belt but has a zip behind that enables you to tuck a few banknotes away. He had to carry his dong in a parcel tied up with newspaper, like two kilos of braised beef.

But the Vietnamese dong is not the least substantial unit of money. One Polish zloty, mentioned earlier, is only half the value of one Vietnamese dong, (i.e., half a speck of dirt).

If you want really big numbers, change your life savings into Intis, the currency of Peru. There are 33,615.3898 Intis to the US dollar. Or try Cordobas, the money of Nicaragua. There are 319,001.985 to one US dollar. A wheelbarrow is a good idea.

A day or two later on that same trip to Vietnam, I had an experience that gave me a fresh point of view on the delicate paper that governs our lives.

I had taken an unplanned diversion into a little rural Vietnamese town which was not on the tourist trail but seemed a good spot for a break. I settled myself in a pavement cafe with a glass of iced coconut milk.

All of a sudden a young girl ran into the restaurant, started pointing at the table next to me and screaming. The two young Vietnamese men sitting at the table looked blankly at her.

The restaurant staff gathered, and then passers-by gathered, and eventually there was a huge crowd gathered around the hysterical girl.

"What is happening?" I asked my driver. "What are they saying?"

"She has lost a great deal of money, which she left in a bag on the table. Twenty-five thousand dong. She is very upset. Poor thing," he said.

"Poor thing," I said.

A few minutes passed, during which she tearfully told her story several more times to the growing crowd.

Then something occurred to me. "Twenty-five thousand dong? How much is that in foreigners' money?" I asked the driver.

"About five dollars," he said.

Of course I did what you or anyone else reading this would do. I took out five dollars and asked the driver to discreetly slip it to the young lady. He did so. There was nothing in the least bit noble about this action — it was clear that destiny had lured a foreigner to that spot for that purpose.

I thought as we drove off: imagine being able to play God for just five dollars.

Now that was easily the biggest bargain of my life.

AT LAST, THE NEW AGE DAWNS IN ASIA

A MASSIVE deposit of new age crystals has been discovered in Caine Road, Hong Kong. Well, when I say "discovered", I mean "located" using methods which seem reliable to the people using them.

You can tell where these things are by looking at churches. Unlike shops and hotels, religious establishments do not appear in clusters since they are usually hostile to each other. When a large number of disparate spiritual centres evolve side by side, this is proof there are good vibrations there.

Anyway, the chap telling me this, a new age businessman I shall call Mr Newman, was very persuasive, and the evidence towered all around us. Caine Road is the site of Caritas, the Roman Catholic centre; the Hong Kong Baptist headquarters; the Buddhist Printing Centre; the Mormons' head office; the Assemblies of God head office; a Hindu centre, and several other temples. Directly west of Caine Road, on Cotton Tree Drive, are St John's Cathedral and St Joseph's Cathedral.

I promptly moved house to Caine Road, and awaited my peaceful evolution into the New Man.

"No, no," said Mr Newman. "It is not who you are that counts, but who speaks through you."

Thus I was introduced to new age concept two: channelling – letting a spirit speak through me. Unfortunately, applied mathematics destroyed this game for me.

Human beings have been around in some shape or other for maybe a million years, or more, depending on which theory you follow. For almost all of that time, they were early hominids and cave dwellers, with a life expectancy of say, 17 to 24 years. Their idea of a fun Saturday night was rooting around for edible roots among droppings from now-extinct ungulates.

Only a tiny, tiny percentage lived in what we may call recent history.

But every time any of Mr Newman's friends did any channelling, he or she got some fascinating warrior king from Egypt, just a couple of thousand years ago or less.

If channelling really worked, a roomful of new age aspirants would be tuning into the available spirits and one would say: "Hey. I'm some kind of repulsive junior cave person."

"So am I," his neighbour would add.

"So am I," everyone in the room would echo.

Anyway, time passed by, and life on noisy, bustling, smelly, run-down Caine Road seemed much too stressful to be a new age experience.

Then, last week, a strange thing happened. It was the first anniversary of my move to the street of deep crystals. I picked up a copy of *Hong Kong Tatler* and discovered that I was on their list as a "Novice New Man". It had worked.

Mr Newman was happy for me, and so was the spirit he was now channelling - a middle manager in the Roman army.

I phoned Ms Rachel Weller, editor of *Hong Kong Tatler,* but was told she had gone home. Where does she live? "Caine Road,"

said her secretary.
    I rest my case. The crystals never lie.

SMART COCKTAILS, STUPID DRINKERS

I knew something serious was wrong from the tone of my wife's voice. "It's Esmerelda," she said. "She's drunk again." Oh no. I slammed the phone down and hurried home. This was a problem that would need all the family brains to solve.

Esmerelda is a large potted houseplant which has lived with us for two years. She has highly responsive leaves: after she is watered, her leaves immediately perk up, moving 45 degrees at a visible rate.

The problem is that the only space big enough for her in our living room is right by a narrow ledge. During parties, drinks tend to fall into her pot.

When this happens, her leaves curl up at the ends the next day. This has happened several times, and her leaves now have a wave in them, like Ronald Reagan's hair just after his hairdresser has finished the morning chiselling session.

"Naughty plant. Naughty. Fancy absorbing all that alcohol," I scolded.

Plant psychologists in the United States claim you should never scold a plant, but I disagree. Politically correct people there don't even call them plants any more — the approved term, I believe, is "vegeto-Americans".

A co-worker tells me it may not be booze. Esmerelda may be drinking too much water. She showed me a newspaper clipping about an air stewardess who appeared to be drunk despite not having touched any alcohol. Doctors discovered she had swallowed four litres of water that day, and it had over-diluted her bodily fluids, making her slur her speech and lose her balance.

Partly in the interests of fearless investigative journalism, but mostly to see if I could save myself an immense amount of hard cash over the next few decades, I did an experiment to check the truth of this. I drank four litres of water in a day.

Only booze-type response: I spent most of the night in the bathroom.

Of course, the best way to save drink money is to restructure one's internal organs and turn them into an alcohol-fermentation plant.

Really. A woman who could do this was also featured in the newspaper. She used to fail breathalyser tests when all she had eaten was a bar of chocolate. Apparently, when she ate chocolate on an empty stomach, it went through a kind of fermentation process and she ended noticeably tipsy. Scientists dubbed it Auto Brewery Syndrome.

This is another experiment I bravely undertook at home, at great personal risk, eating only chocolate for 12 hours.

Sole booze-type response: nausea.

Anyway, I have latterly discovered that drinking alcohol is passe. People in Japan, Hong Kong and Thailand are into a new thing: drinking themselves extra-sober. They take cocktails of things called "smart drugs".

Users claim they have amazing effect on your thought patterns, making them as sharp as that of a teenager. They obviously don't know the same teenagers we do.

The parties of the near future, I am told, will be divided into people drinking alcohol, and thus becoming increasingly dopey, and people taking smart cocktails and thus becoming ever more infuriatingly lucid.

Booze-drinker: Hic. Who wantsh a fight?

Smartie: Not me. I feel like reciting the Iliad in its original Greek. Anyone care to listen?

Booze-drinker: Shaddup. Who do you think you are?

Smartie: Do you mean my Id, my Ego, my past life, or the spirit that channels through me?

Boozer punches Smartie.

Smartie gets up, grabs a napkin, and writes out a three-page indictment for assault from memory.

I can tell you one thing, though. When smart cocktails become de rigueur in Asia, I am going to move Esmerelda into the bathroom. If there is one thing I can't stand when I'm drinking, it's pieces of decorative vegetation displaying intellectual superiority.

HEADHUNTING FOR REAL HEADS

So there I was, sitting in the Sarawak jungle, chatting to a headhunter called Ranggal.

Unlike headhunters in other Asian cities, Ranggal did his executive outplacement work using a large knife called a parang.

One clutches the hair of the executive to be despatched. One gives two sharp blows to the neck. One then punches a hole in the skull, pulls out a piece of warm brain, and eats it. This prevents the spirit from haunting one afterward.

It was dusk, and we were in a wooden longhouse (a shack on stilts) drinking tuak, a fermented rice wine. We had travelled by canoe down a winding jungle river to get there.

Suddenly there was a tiny blue glimmer of light visible through the slatted walls of the neighbouring longhouse. Then we heard some electronic beeping noises. Beeping? In a rainforest, miles from civilisation? I crept over to have a look.

A Chinese businessman was punching numbers into a

mobile telephone. This is not a joke. Nor was it a hallucination caused by the tuak.

The caller turned out to be a Mr Yap, a Cantonese-Hokkien businessman working as a car salesman in the region.

"How can a mobile phone work so far from any cellular transmitting stations?" I asked.

"Oh no problem," said Mr Yap, pointing to a box in his bag, to which the telephone was linked. "This is a transmitter that sends signals to a satellite."

Are there really customers for cars in the jungle?

Yes, even in one of the world's least-explored rainforests, fast cars are popular. They are transported to isolated townships via the river.

A few years ago, an explorer travelled to the town of Kapit in the interior of Sarawak and reported finding a fleet of Fords and Toyotas parked there.

This was despite the fact that the town only had two miles of road.

When I got back to Hong Kong, I bumped into aviation consultant Robert Christensen, who had also been trekking through the jungles of Sarawak. He had travelled by foot through the steamy rainforest into the interior. After several days slashing through thick foliage, he came upon a tiny settlement, a trading post called Nga Dia.

In the heart of it was an ice cream parlour.

And yes, it was run by a Chinese businessman. The entrepreneur had imported an ice-cream machine and a power generator from Sweden and brought it up the Rajan River by longboat.

Verily, the sun never sets on the Chinese entrepreneur.

MADE IN ASIA: TOMORROW'S PRODUCTS – TOMORROW

On a bender: Popped into the Industrial Tools Trade Show in the Hong Kong convention centre.

The most intriguingly named organisation in the guidebook was the "Hong Kong Mould and Die Council". We went to find them. This turned out to be not a group of decomposing cadavers, but a gang of machine enthusiasts.

There was even a magazine available called *Die and Mould*, possibly the least appealing title for a periodical we have ever encountered.

The member of government officiating, Director of Industry T. H. Barma, politely strolled around and nodded at the machines, but it was hard to guess what each pile of metal did. One had to guess from the names.

Wing Li Machinery handles a "Horizontal bender", a term with which we are familiar, albeit it in a markedly different context.

Shih Hsing Enterprise Co had a Bun Moulding Machine.

According to the show guidebook, this had an "astonishing special function". The whole idea seemed astonishing to us.

Pun Teh Industrial had a "Quick Coupler", which sounded fun, although we could not work out how two people would get in it.

On firm claimed to be a "slag supplier".

We hate to be cynical, but these always go down well at international trade shows.

Rocky venture: At the International Audio-Visual Show, a firm called Ligitek was demonstrating a system that puts subtitles on films. When we arrived they switched on one of the *Rocky* movies.

On the screen, a wrestler approached Sylvester Stallone. "Ha ha ha!" said the wrestler.

"HA HA HA" said the English subtitles.

"HAA HAA HAA" said the Chinese subtitles in Chinese characters.

How could we ever have enjoyed *Rocky* without this obviously essential device?

In the photographic section, a firm called Tamron was selling Fotovix III, a gadget that enables you to watch your own still photographs on television.

This is ideal for people who find Hong Kong television too mentally stimulating, and want something a bit duller. Such people may exist, but frankly, we doubt it.

A sock in the face: Now available in Asia: outer-space socks. Debra Richardson of Standard Chartered Bank bought a pair of "ADragon" brand men's cotton socks with small ceramic nodules sewn into the cloth.

Sound uncomfortable? It's worth it when you hear some of the attributes of this remarkable item of footwear, designed for astronauts.

"ADragon socks meet all the requirements of underwears," says the packaging. First, "the surface of the fibre is specially treated with the highest quality flavour". Second, they are "processed with the living body activation material". Third, "anti-sperm material is contained". Fourth, they are "very effectable for menstruation of women".

ADragon, a South Korean company, claims that the bioceramics contained in the socks were invented by NASA. But since they have such wide applications, the package includes a diagram of the internal organs of the human body.

Good as underwear? Full of flavour? Anti-sperm? Ideal for menstruation? Debra said: "One has to ask: whereabouts on the body is one supposed to wear these socks?"

We should think they work very well pulled over the eyes of people who buy them, Debra.

Computer graphics: Staff at Star Computers wanted to show how accurate their colour scanning machine was.

So they ran off a few banknotes with it.

A young lady from the firm was happily sticking the results on the wall when we arrived at the Computer Trade Fair. They looked almost good enough to spend. She had made copies of various notes, including HK$100, HK$50, US$100, US$50 and some large denomination yen.

It is certainly a wonderful machine. If Star Computers would lend it to us for a few hours, we would happily buy one from them — and we'll pay cash (which may still be warm).

● Meanwhile, there was great excitement in the "plotters" section. Plotters are computer attachments which draw lines, graphs or other graphics with super-high micro-fine precision.

Someone at Mutoh Industries has just worked out how to connect high-precision plotters with those fashionable new circuits called "fuzzy logic".

Have the people at Mutoh Industries really thought this one through?

Drink yourself sober: Nipped into China Science Week show at the China Resources Building's exhibition hall in Wan Chai, Hong Kong. It is clear that the boffins over the border are way ahead of everyone else.

Some of the items on show:

1. *Aidsconin.*
This is a box containing vials of liquid which "Prevents and Cures AIDS". It is pronounced AIDS-Con-In. Hmm.

2. *Jiuxian Sober-Up Tea.* The package says: "This product is good at drunkenness, sottishness and abnormal gait."

3. *Gunpowder Tea.* A drink with a real kick to it.

4. *Zhuangyuan Brand Magic Comb for Invigorating Mind.* Just give your hair a quick comb and suddenly you are more intelligent. (We reckon this product is grossly unfair to bald people.)

5. *Model Activating Brain and Opening Orifices Stimulation Instruments.* We've never heard them called that before.

6. *Natural Decreasing Fat Bag.* This sounded interesting, so we went to stall C7, but we could not find her anywhere.

7. *Multi-Efficacious Perfume: Mouldproof and Insectofungicide.* This is extremely useful for the many of us with mould, insects and fungus growing underneath our ears.

In another corner we found vegetables for married people. The catalogue says: "Dragon Vegetable is a secret recipe of imperial court of Oing Dynasty for kink. It has evidently strong masculinity result."

How strong do they mean? That Oing Dynasty didn't last long, did it? One almost never hears about it.

For wives, there is the Phoenix Vegetable. "It changes appearance from woman's inner body. It may get the woman's eye bright, get face bright red, get skin bright-coloured and get winkles disappear."

Isn't a winkle a type of coastal mollusc? Not many Asian women are plagued by winkles, thank goodness.

Thick-skinned: Received a fascinating letter containing a press release headlined: "Taiping Industries Ltd Launches a Revolutionary Du Pont Product: Super-Strong, Lightweight, Moisture-Proof Envelopes."

The text: "Taiping Industries Ltd is now offering a complete line of business envelopes made from the incredible material TYVEK. Because envelopes made of TYVEK are about half the weight of their paper equivalents and twice as strong they are ideal for mailing."

It came in brown manilla.

Mulled wine or mould wine?: Scientists in Sichuan province have managed to make booze out of fungus, the *China Daily* reported. The technique has apparently won a state gold prize for new patent products.

"Many internationally renowned experts hailed the invention as a great contribution to mankind," it says. "Liquor made in this way is said to be nutritious."

● Some suggestions for names of cocktails to be made from fungi-booze:
Harvey Wallgrowth
Between The Toes.

Chateau Mocca: Talking of booze, a firm in Hainan province has just invented a new product called Coffee Wine. Boffins at the Changmai Coffee Plant have brewed it from coffee beans and claim it is wonderful.

"The plant plans to produce 400 tons of the wine annually,"

says the *China Daily*.

It does not say whether drinking it will keep you awake or put you to sleep.

Worst biological knowledge: John Adams of P & O Containers was browsing in Stanley Market, when he found a shop selling garments emblazoned with the words "BUM EQUIPMENT".

Curiously, they are garments designed for the upper body. Maybe it is a range of exporter designer garments targeted at American tramps?

Most mysterious brochure: Beancounter Tony Nedderman sent us a brochure for ITWeek, a hi-tech trade show scheduled for August in Hong Kong. The term IT (information technology) lends itself wonderfully to innuendo. For example, the show includes a demonstration of "how the Police Force uses IT to increase efficiency".

Mr Nedderman's covering letter said:
RE: IT.
Dear Lai See,
You are always talking about IT.
I assume you are not getting enough of IT.
(Though some people say you are full of IT.)

Materialistic: Spotted a sign on Wan Chai Road: The Chinese Muslin Cultural and Fraternal Association Welfare Centre.

Muslin is a very nice type of fabric, but we are surprised that there are enthusiasts around who have actually started a club.

What do they sit around and talk about? Texture and washability? Cloth roll of the week?

Most unusual location for a cellular phone transmitter: Those blasted new CT2 mini-phones are popping up everywhere. A gleaming, fluorescent Telepoint sign has just appeared dangling from a shop half-way up Shing Wong Street in Western district, not far from where the flag was first planted in Hong Kong.

Shing Wong Street is really an old "village" on an stone staircase, similar to Ladder Street. There is no access for vehicles.

Charming but toothless old ladies in pyjamas sit on stools telling stories to each other. The buildings are crumbling, wood-framed structures that were sold off-plan when God was a small boy.

You don't get a lot of yuppies there.

Worst-named fax machine: At Hong Kong Telecom's media quiz, held in Mad Dogs pub, freelance writer Gerry O'Kane won a combined telephone, answering machine and fax, called a Tamfax.

"It's very nice," said Gerry, glancing sidelong at the name of the machine. "But are you sure it is not for a woman?"

Most bizarre product ideas: These were sent in by readers to Japanese magazine *Direct Mail Life:*

● A giant Swiss army knife for gardening, which features a hoe, rake and shovel.

● Dress shoes with no soles for the man who wants to enjoy the natural feel of walking on grass while maintaining a proper corporate image.

Best Chinese wine: Visitors to Guangdong often return with tales of the broad range of animal life consumed there.

Dr Ronald Leung of Des Voeux Road popped into the Shenzhen Bay Hotel for a drink, where the menu offered him "Mouse Wine", available by the glass.

"I opted for the iced coffee," said Dr Leung.

Presumably you drink Mouse Wine to wash down the domestic pets on sale in food markets elsewhere in Guangdong.

Meanwhile, Martyn Uttley of Shouson Hill tells us that he has tried the "Mouse Wine" offered in Shenzhen.

"I much prefer gin and tonic with lemming," he said. "Especially if served with rat-atouille."

Yummiest frank: On sale among the weird and wonderful items in the food department of Japanese store Seibu, Hong Kong: "Litter Weiners".

Surely Seibu is taking this recycling business too far?

Best gadget for corporate espionage agents: Fred Wahl of Dinner For Six Ltd received a tempting offer from Diners Club — a compact desktop shredder for only HK$396.

The text says: "Just flip the switch and it will quickly shred any discarded document. And just in case, it also has a reverse switch."

"Fantastic," enthused Fred. "A device that can unshred paper."

Corporate espionage agents are advised to buy one and keep it permanently on reverse.

Spit and polish: Dreamgirl leans towards your neck and inhales deeply. "Mmm. You smell great," she breathes.

"Bug spittle," you reply. She swoons into your arms, overcome with sensual delight.

It's the new perfume sensation: saliva from an insect related to the mealy bug. We may all be splashing this stuff on our necks soon, and some of us have already started.

Bug saliva has a special effect on normal perfume, we learned from an exhibitor at Cosmetics, Hair and Beauty 92, a Hong Kong trade fair.

But don't go trying to goad ants into gobbing at you. The spitball has to be from *lacifer lacca*, a tiny red-brown creature that starts off like a grub, and ends up like an ant. A chemical called ambrettolide is extracted from the spittle. It increases the strength and duration of the perfume's "top note" – the primary aroma.

The "lac" bug is found mainly in north India and Thailand, and the stuff is marketed by an Indian firm called Okhla Chemicals.

We cannot help but wonder how this was discovered.

A perfume industry executive must have said to his wife one day: "You smell good today."

To which she must have replied: "Funny. You always say that when bugs spit in my face."

Doesn't add up: Picked up a delicious portion of Knabber Nossi (slogan: "The unpronounceable Sausage Snack") this week.

"Not less than 100 per cent meat" says the package.

It also lists the ingredients: "Beef, pork fat, fresh garlic, salt, spices, flavour enhancer: E621, emulsifier: diphosphate, antidoxant: ascorbic acid, preservative: sodium nitrate."

Are these all types of meat?

How many legs does an E621 have?

Card car: Volvo is unveiling its "talking car" at the Hong Kong Hilton Ballroom. The announcement says "it is an entirely new car, created from a blank sheet of paper".

Oh well, it's probably cheaper than metal.

On show will be the first Volvo "with curves", says the announcement.

They obviously don't remember the girls of Club Volvo, the former Tsim Sha Tsui East hostess bar. They had curves.

A message to cabbies: Taxi drivers, are some of your passengers a real pain in the neck? Now you can give them a real pain somewhere else.

You can turn your taxi's passenger seats into electric chairs on wheels.

All you need is a machine developed by the Shijiazhuang Electrical Appliance Factory of China.

You stick the main device inside the passenger seat. A small wire leads into the driver's section, hooked up to a switch discreetly placed on the steering wheel.

Then sit back and enjoy the ride. As soon as the passenger starts to get stroppy, flick the switch and – ZZZAAAPPPPP!

The device, which has received a patent in China, is being marketed as a means to lower the number of taxi robberies.

But one cannot help but worry what would happen if it got into the hands of some of the wide boys that drive taxis in Hong Kong. The time cannot be far away when they start demanding a "No Electrocution Surcharge".

Bags of fun: There was an attempted crime at the Hong Kong Jewellery Trade Fair that went completely unreported. We know, because we committed it.

At a stall on the western side of the hall, Lambert Wong of Golden Rise Development was selling high security leather briefcases. These things are enormous fun. If you owned one, you would pray daily for someone to steal it.

It looks like an innocent black leather attache case. But as soon as the owner notices it has gone, he or she presses a little button on a small black box.

Pow! The thief gets a nasty electric shock, screams and drops the bag, and an alarm goes off.

It's a real shocker. "Watch this," said Mr Wong and touched the case with a thin piece of metal. There was a flash of sparks and a crackling noise.

"Go on, steal it," said Mr Wong. "I'll turn the shocker off."

In the interests of product testing, Lai See grabbed the HK$6,000 bag and raced off with it. We had just reached the convention centre doors when Mr Wong pressed his button and the alarm went off.

Due to amazing stupidity on the part of this columnist, this occurred close to where the heavily armed security guards stood. Fortunately, good sense prevailed and they were dissuaded from filling us full of holes.

We returned the bag to Mr Wong. "Isn't it dangerous?" we asked.

"No," he said. He admitted that he himself had accidentally pressed the shocker "on" button and touched the case.

"I'm still alive," he assured us.

A sensitive sheath for the dirty Mac brigade: Donning a pair of thick spectacles, we slid unnoticed into a herd of nerds stampeding into Nerd Heaven: the MacWorld Exposition, at the Convention Centre in Wan Chai.

On the stand of Nuts Technologies, there were some computers with a device on top which looked suspiciously like an eye. We peered into one, and a chap at the other end of the room suddenly flinched as if he had seen something horrible.

In fact the eye-shaped thing WAS an eye. The chap opposite had just seen us.

We pressed a button, and we could see a shocking close-up of him looking shocked at having seen us. Hours of fun.

The proprietors of this wonderful but terrifying video-phone device, Stetson and Christine Chung, are getting lots of orders for it.

In another corner of the theatre, a firm called Alpha Pioneer was selling a type of condom. Feeling brave, we actually tried one out, right there in the exhibition hall. Honest. It worked very well.

You pick up this HK$150 computer condom, called SafeSkin, and slide it over a computer keyboard. It is an ultra-thin and ultra-sensitive cover. The keyboard was placed under a running tap, and continued to work perfectly, and you really can't feel the layer of plastic when you type.

We don't have a running tap over our keyboard at home, but

others may do.

Much of the rest of the show is concerned with abstruse applications of desktop publishing. In the midst of these was a stand with a huge banner showing its name: "Linotype-Hell".

This in fact is the name of a product, but it could really apply to most of the show.

Most significant Asian trade fair sight: David Gosling, managing director of Avon, popped into the Hong Kong Toy Fair. The stall that caught his eye was stand 5PO3: Menq Ho Morality Co, from Taiwan.

"The stand shelves and tables were absolutely bare and the salesman was fast asleep," said Mr Gosling.

Rather telling.

CAR-OKE FOR BEGINNERS

Roger Eastham of 22 North Ltd, a shop in Marina Cove, Hong Kong, jumped into a taxi. "I was greeted by the sound of a cat being disembowelled, amplified 25 times," he said afterwards.

He had leaned forward to ask the taxi driver to change channels. But then he realised the wailing noise did not come from the radio, but from the CB communicator.

The *diksi* -driver explained that the noise was Sai Kung's top taxi-driving harmonica player, doing a live performance on the CB.

"Inspired by the apparent success of the harmonic player, the driver burst into what I guess can only be described as a song," said Roger, his eyes widening with terror at the painful memory.

Before he could leap out of the window, Mr Eastham found himself being driven along accompanied by a duet. The singing came from his driver and the backing from the unseen harmonic player over in taxi number 628.

"For the rest of the trip, the cabbie seemed more intent on hitting 'C' flat than third gear," said Mr Eastham.

"Do the Japanese realise the market potential for interactive group car CB stereo systems?" he asked. "I hope not."

● A few days later, advertising man Hans Ebert stepped into a taxi outside the Sun Hung Kai Centre and heard the warning signs: backing music through the CB transmitter.

A terrifying realisation came upon him: he too was in a karaoke kab.

The taxi promptly ran into a traffic jam.

"Pleeeese release me, let me go, for Ieeiiiii don't love you any more," wailed the cabbie.

Hans, who also no longer felt the same warmth for the driver, reached for the door, preferring to risk death on the expressway, but it was locked.

The driver's next number was *Stand By Me*, after which he got stuck into a song the chorus of which was: "Sheets for my sheet."

The cabbie turned around and peered at Mr Ebert's generous endowment of hair.

"Are you a musician?" he asked. "What means 'Sheets for my sheet'?"

Hans explained, and slowly became friendly with the songster. The car eventually pulled up at Hans' home in Jardine's Lookout with the two of them singing in harmony: "Sheets for my sheet, sugar for my honey."

"There's got to be money in it," Hans told us. "Cassettes for taxi drivers. These are lonely guys. They drive around all day by themselves. You could even slot in advertisements between the tracks."

We left him dialling the numbers of his friends at Polygram to issue some albums.

In the meantime, here are some suggestions for the first taxi album (on the Carcophony label):

For New Territories drivers: *24 hours from Tai Po.*
For tunnel drivers: *All My Life's a Circle.*
For people stuck in the Friday night queues on Gloucester Road:
All Night Long.
I Could Write a Book.
In The Year 2525.
Etc, etc.

La la land: Readers have sent in suggestions for hot hits for karaoke kabs.

From Betty Brown of Wan Chai, for trips to Hong Kong University: *What Kind of Pokfulam I?*

From a broker, for use by nervous executives when visiting compliance officer Paul Phenix at the Hong Kong stock exchange: *By the Time I Get to Phenix.*

The night before, she recommends *24 Hours to Ulcer.*

For Nikkei analysts in Japan: *I Can't Tell the Bottom From the Top.*

Dog Star: Anna McLaughlin of Discovery Bay took her two collie dogs, Casey and Hugo, to play with sick children in a Hong Kong island hospital, as part of the Doctor Dog programme.

On her way back, she stepped into a cab and discovered, yes, that it too was a ... karaoke kab!

On went the backing music and the car was soon wobbling down the highway with the cabbie wailing at the top of his voice to Canto-pop hits.

Anna, who insists she cannot sing, kept quiet in the back. The curious dogs listened intently, with their ears and noses up.

Suddenly, Casey the collie opened his mouth and said: "Hooowwwwll." Then Hugo joined in. "Wooooooooo."

Then both dogs decided to sing along.

The delighted cabbie wound down the windows to share this extraordinary mobile opera with the world, as they travelled through streets full of shocked pedestrians.

When the car arrived at Blake Pier, Casey and Hugo decided they liked karaoke and did not want to leave the taxi. "They would happily have driven around all day singing Canto-pop hits with this driver," said Anna.

The dogs had sung themselves hoarse and she had to give them throat lozenges when they got home.

Wonder if that TVB "Search For a Star" contest is still open?

Kraziest Karaoke Kulture: Japanese firm Pioneer has launched an interior karaoke system which will fit any private car. LA-style freeway shootings will no doubt follow shortly. (Acceptable plea: gross provocation.)

The music is piped in for *six hours* without a break.

The driver is supplied with a remote control device which can be used to switch it off, in case the singing is so intense or cacophonic that it becomes a hazard to safe motoring (for instance, if someone selects *Feelings*).

● Suggested songs for Car-oke in Hong Kong:

Jammin' ("We're jammin' until the break of day") for use in Nathan Road.

Long and Winding Road for Wong Nei Chung Gap.

Get Off of My Cloud for Lugard Road, the Peak.

I'll Be Home For Christmas for users of the Lion Rock Tunnel. (Optimistic ones, that is.)

Driven to distraction: Climbed gingerly into the most frightening car in the world at a trade show. It was a slick white Mercedes on display at the International Audio-Visual Show at the convention centre in Hong Kong. In the middle of the dashboard was a little rectangular box, which looked like an innocent car radio.

But it wasn't. Sitting next to us was Nelson Woo of TAC Automobile of Happy Valley, who pressed the "on" button.

Suddenly the box slid out of the dashboard and angled itself up to reveal a television screen.

We reached for the hand-brake — and it came off in our hands. Had we broken it? No. The stick-like device between the seats was a hand-held microphone.

Yes. This was the ultimate karaoke car.

Nelson pressed another button. Lyrics appeared on the television screen and deafening music thundered out of 11 hidden speakers around the inside of the vehicle.

He fiddled with a remote control. Suddenly our buttocks and naughty bits started to pulsate. Oh no! We seemed to be having some sort of embarrassing physiological reaction!

Thankfully this was not the case.

Mr Woo explained that he had just pressed the "surround sound" button. This made the whole car — and both of us — throb organically to the music.

The whole system costs HK$80,000 to HK$110,000, plus the price of the car.

Surely people were not throbbing around Hong Kong, singing to their passengers?

"Oh yes," said Nelson. "We've already sold about 20."

You have been warned. If there was ever an excuse not to accept lifts from strangers, this is it.

kars join the banned: Slunk back into the International Audio-Visual Show yesterday to find that the constabulary had swooped on the karaoke-kar.

The officer showed staff at TAC Automobile Ltd a law saying you cannot have television in the driver's line of sight.

"This isn't television," boss Thomas Woo argued. "These pictures come from a karaoke player."

There was an uneasy truce.

There is not yet a set of statutes on karaoke, a lawyer tells us, but the time will come. Eventually a prosecutor will bring it up in court, and some old judge will say: "Karaoke? Is that some sort of wireless gramophonic device? Would counsel kindly demonstrate?"

You will never see a courtroom empty so fast.

ADVENTURES IN THE PROPERTY TRADE

"Property traders are the most boring people in the world," he said, with an air of abrupt finality.

There was a chorus of gasps of amazement.

Why? Because, dear reader, the man who made the above preposterous statement was an ACCOUNTANT.

Yes, that's right, a member of that profession famed throughout the galaxy for the way its adherents continually redefine the frontiers of tedium.

When I had finished making my chorus of gasps of amazement (I had to do them all, since there were only the two of us at the bar that night), I remonstrated with him in no uncertain fashion.

"Steady on," I said. "May I remind you that you yourself, are, in fact, an accountant."

"Rubbish," he said. "When was the last time you heard someone describe themselves as an accountant? These days, we are all 'financial directors' or 'troubleshooters' or even 'bagmen'. Never accountants. When was the last time you read a novel in which the protagonist was in the real estate business? You get courtroom thrillers, detective books, journalism books, books about spies and diplomats, etc etc. But when is the good guy ever in real estate? Name one instance."

There's lots of fiction in which property people appear, I said. In *Gremlins II* there is a real estate developer called "Clamp", based on a certain Mr Trump.

"There are lots of books and films in which property developers are the bad guys," he said. "But I bet there aren't any in which they are the good guys."

Mulling this over after a few days, I realised that he was right. Property dealers are never beatified in thrillers. I have no idea why.

I did check out some books in the local bookshop which had titles suggesting that they were about property, such as *The L-Shaped Room, Hotel du Lac* and *The Ebony Tower*. Not a single one turned out to be about real estate.

To set this deficiency to rights, we hereby present something a bit different: the first mini-thriller written about, and for, the long-suffering, hardworking foot-soldiers of real estate.

CHAPTER ONE
Scene: a stockbroker's office in Tokyo

Pilbeam picked up the monitor from his desk, and, ripping it from the wires which held it in place, planted it squarely in the waste bin.

"I've jolly well had enough of the stock market business," he said. "I want to do something that will make me more money for less work."

His companion, a wiley moneyman called Lee who had a

taste for expensive Italian suits, looked up from the newspaper he was reading. "You do sod-all anyway."

"Don't nit-pick," spat Pilbeam.

"I've got just the thing," said Lee. "Look at this: 'New Development in the Property Industry: Entrepreneurs Make Millions Out of Reversion Scheme'."

"What's that?" asked Pilbeam, who had lost much of his ability to think through having worked as a stockbroker for several years.

Lee clucked his tongue with impatience. "Reversion is a scheme where old people who are just about to die sell you their flats for practically nothing — well, half price, shall we say. Then they live it up for their autumn years with the cash you have given them, and when they die, the house is yours to sell for a guaranteed profit."

"Where are they doing it?" asked Pilbeam.

"In the north of England," said Lee, dialling the number of the property firm.

Lee was used to making deals on the phone. He quickly traced the decision maker in the firm and said: "Yes, I'm talking about the reversion scheme for the retired people's houses in the town of Little Muchness, South Yorkshire. We want to buy them. Yes. ALL of them."

CHAPTER TWO
Scene: a village in Yorkshire. Our two heroes are having a drink at a pub called the Frog and Carbuncle.

"We've been cheated," growled Lee into his pint of Ruddles Ale. "And we don't even have any decent booze to drown our sorrows with. Don't they have any REAL beer here, such as Sapporro Dry?"

"I don't understand," said Pilbeam. "The houses look okay to me."

"It's not the houses that are the problem. It's the people. We've been deluded into buying the dwelling places of the Little Muchness Athletic Ex-Servicemen's Retirees Club. These guys have all just retired early. They'll probably live another 40 years. We'll be pensioners before we get the houses which we've just paid for."

"Oh," said Pilbeam. "I see. What shall we do while we are waiting?"

"You fool," said Lee. "We can't just pass the time for 40 years until they pop off. We'll just have to hurry along their deaths a little bit. I've got a plan . . .'

CHAPTER THREE
It is midnight in the village.

Lee and Pilbeam are sneaking through the undergrowth outside the Little Muchness Athletic Ex-Servicemen's Retirees Club, where members are entertaining themselves by playing catch with a Fiat Uno. The two property buyers are clutching a bomb which they plan to detonate and throw through the window.

"This is a much better idea than sitting around and waiting for people to die," said Lee, lighting the bomb. "This way the whole village becomes ours in five minutes time."

Just then, they are blinded by a dazzling beam from a searchlight. They hear a voice say: "Please come along quietly with us." Then follows the click of handcuffs.

CHAPTER FOUR
Scene: A real estate office in Yorkshire, where a tall, striking property man is talking to the chief of police.

"It worked a treat," said the policeman.

"Didn't I tell you it would," said the property man, an

incredibly handsome and clever man, called John Brilliant. "They never notice the clause in the small print which says that where the owner of the property tries to murder the sitting tenant, the house will return to its original owner and all monies paid will be forfeited."

"You are doing a grand job of bringing millions of pounds of investment into Yorkshire, Mr Brilliant, Sir," said the policeman.

"I'm doing it for the good of the community," replied the property man, his sincerity and honesty shining from his clear blue eyes. "Real estate people don't make the headlines as much as some people, but that doesn't mean our hearts aren't in the right place."

The police chief, overcome by this speech, pretends he has something in his eye.

But real estate swashbuckler John Brilliant will not rest on his laurels. He says: "No time to slack. Business is business. Where shall we place the 'reversion' advertisement next? Taiwan? Texas?"

THE END

What's that? Did someone say it wasn't believable? That property people tend to be small and wizened and insincere, and hate to take risks?

Nonsense. I'll have you know that the above story is based on a conversation I had with an Asian property developer, who was thinking about putting into operation some sort of offbeat investment scheme to attract dollars into needy areas, such as the local community, his bank account, and so on.

Sadly, he never actually put any such a plan into action.
He used to be an accountant.

BEAUTIFUL HOMES AND GARDENS WITH FUNNY SHAPED HEDGES

OH BOY! I'm nearly famous. I have just learned that the home of my very own next-door neighbour is being featured in a glossy monthly magazine. I can hardly believe it.

You know the sort of thing I mean. Those fat consumer mags with titles such as *Beautiful Homes and Gardens With Funny Shaped Hedges Monthly.*

A mutual friend told me about my neighbour's good fortune, and I believe I detected a tinge of jealousy in his words.

"Why that no-good over-paid hedonist Greenstreet is having his ludicrously extravagant palace featured in some dumb magazine this month. I can't believe the editors have such a crass lack of taste."

Dear reader, I do not want you to think the present writer lives in the lap of luxury. He lives in a small poky flat more or less next to a luxurious block full of huge apartments. The gentleman being featured in the magazine, Hongkong celebrity Greenstreet Kan, bought TWO of the huge apartments and knocked down the wall between them.

What makes a flat suitable for featuring in a colour spread?

Studying the magazine, I noted the following points:

1. The flat must look as if no human being has ever been near it.

2. The seating must look artistic (ie, uncomfortable).

3. The owner must have a grand piano and a fluffy white cat.

There is always a quote from the owner on the lines of: "I spent hours looking for Louis 15th teak-toned Poggenpohl fittings that would match my genuine Eritrean Wedgewood display case."

Mulling this over, we decided that these magazines really do not take enough risks. Therefore, we would like to present a special feature:

REGULAR FEATURES WE WOULD LIKE TO SEE IN A "BEAUTIFUL HOUSE" TYPE MAGAZINE.

1. A feature called REAL PEOPLE'S HOMES, or perhaps, WARTS 'N' ALL.

You brief a commando-style team of photographer and interviewer, and send them to the district or city you want featured.

They then burst unannounced into the home of Mr and Mrs Average, and say: "Freeze. This is a Photo Opportunity."

The resultant feature would be something like this:

Pic. 1. A living room which is a repulsive shade of salmon on one side, and has peeling wallpaper on the other. On the wall is a plastic-framed print of a small boy with a tear coming from one eye. In the middle of the sofa is a surprised-looking couple eating dinner on their laps and watching television.

Caption: "Er. We chose salmon for the walls because the

wife's brother managed to get a job lot of it cheap. The skirting board is in mushroom, because there was some left in a tin we found under the sink. Er."

Pic 2. The bedroom. There is an enormous pile of dirty washing on the bed, which is unmade. There are very obvious blotches of damp on the walls. There is a mirror on the ceiling.

Caption: "Er. The grey-green effect on the walls is actually made by damp from a leak from the flat upstairs. But we decided to leave it, because it looked a bit like that posh textured effect that some people have. The mirror on the ceiling? Er. We saw it on a James Bond movie once and went straight out and had it done. We're very original and spontaneous like that, the wife and I."

Pic 3. The kitchen. A huge pile of dirty dishes rises from the sink. Piles of used pots and pans line all surfaces.

Caption: "Er. We like it to look 'lived-in'."

2. Then we would like to see a regular monthly column called: BLOW THE WHISTLE ON YOUR FRIENDS, or perhaps TALK ABOUT BAD TASTE.

The introductory blurb would say:

Have you ever been invited to someone's house, and found it difficult to keep yourself from laughing out loud, because the decor is so horrible? Now is your chance to let off steam. Yes, send all the details to Blow The Whistle On Your Friends, and we will fearlessly print the whole, horrible, hideous, sordid TRUTH.

Are you reading this, Mr and Mrs Goop of Baghdad Terrace, Singapore?

No less than three of your dinner guests anonymously nominated you for Dump of the Month. Here are their comments:

"Your revolting colour schemes made me feel sick. The revolting food finished the job."

"The portrait of your cross-eyed grandmother hanging in the bathroom was the best laugh I've had in months."

"How did you get your walls stippled? Did your previous guests throw their dinners at it?"

3. Lastly, we would like to see a gardening column called LOOK WHAT THEY'VE DONE TO MY HEDGE, MA, or perhaps IT'S MEANT TO BE A WHAT?

Readers are invited to send in photographs of topiary works in progress. Other readers would then write in and suggest what they think the hedges look like.

I myself have a photograph I could enter for this particular contest. My cousin, a highly ambitious gardener, once tried to recreate a scene from the classic Marilyn Monroe film *The Seven-Year Itch* entirely in privet.

I was with him at a bar on the day he showed a picture of it to another gardening expert. "What do you think it looks like?" he asked.

The reply: "It looks like a small, slightly damaged privet hedge."

If any editors of "Good Homemaker"-type magazines are reading this, you are welcome to steal these ideas.

But on one condition. The magazine must guarantee that Your Humble Narrator will never open his door to find a commando-style team of magazine staff standing on the doorstep saying: "Freeze. This is a Photo Opportunity."

TOYS FOR MODERN CHILDREN AND OTHER DANGEROUSLY DERANGED LUNATICS

It ain't me babe: Playmates is going to try and regain its profit growth with some hot new toys including Baby Burpy, we learned from studying its new catalogue.

Baby Burpy is a new doll which drinks heavily, gets noticeably fatter, and then gives a loud belch when hugged.

Research by Playmates has shown that this is what females want.

Funny. Mrs Lai See never seems to appreciate this kind of behaviour.

Wet ones: Want to know the new trend in children's toys? Realistic body fluids.

To anyone reading this over breakfast: DO NOT READ FURTHER. In fact, you had better skip this whole chapter.

Other toy makers are opting for icky, gross, bizarre themes following the success of Playmates' Ninja Turtles.

Since the majority of the world's toys are made in this

region, we thought you should know what is being produced behind factory walls.

Hasbro will bid for market share with Monster Face. This is a plastic head which comes with super-realistic greenish mucus. You can make the mucus ooze from his nose or spew from his mouth.

Tyco is after the female market with Magic Potty Baby. When you put dolly on the potty, she makes a realistic "tinkle" sound and emits a yellow urine-like fluid from a, er, suitable opening. The Tyco package includes a supply of real working toilet paper. We are not making this up.

We warn you now: the next generation of kids is going to be pretty weird. In comparison, Michael Jackson is going to look like Mr Boring, John Major.

Boldly lunching where no man has lunched before: Paul Rivers and Steve Temkin have just come back from New Orleans. The likely lads were there at a trade fair representing Pam and Frank, the Hong Kong sports bag firm.

They caused a stir with the firm's latest (and grossest) product. These are life-size heads of characters from *Star Trek*. But open up the top of their skulls and you find − your lunch.

Apparently research has shown that eating out of a severed head is considered the height of good taste for modern children. No doubt Calvin of the *Calvin and Hobbes* cartoon was among those interviewed.

Barbie crew: Sigmund Freud would love what the toy industry is now doing. A new product in the doll category is "Twins", consisting of two dolls that giggle when they are together and cry when they are apart. Slip both dolls a pacifier and they promise to be silent. Give only one a rubber nipple to suck on, though, and the other twin howls.

Yes, now your dolls can go through sibling trauma, just like you did.

What next? Oedipus baby dolls from Mattel which kill Ken before climbing into Barbie's bedroom?

Start your yuplet young: Street-smart toys are all the rage at the Hong Kong Toys and Games Fair.

Foster your baby-yuplet's interest in gadgets with My First Toy Video Camera by Fred's Industrial Co of Kwun Tong or a folding CT-2 style mobile phone from Onoeman of Tsim Sha Tsui.

Initiate your yuplet into the popular couch potato lifestyle with a baby toy operated with a real working remote control from Rockapetta Industrial of Kowloon Bay. He or she just clutches the remote control and presses a button using the thumb. "You can use it to teach them how to use a VCR," enthused production manager Raymond Tsui.

Are the baby's karaoke skills up to scratch? Buy Karaoke Kid, a Videotech stand-alone karaoke set with all the same functions as daddy's big flash Japanese one.

Teach your yuplet modern office politics, with arguing toys from Safe Treasure of Tsuen Wan. One repeats: "Cough, cough, cough. No smoking." The other replies with a string of obscenities.

Train baby for business lunches with a battery-operated plate of raw fish by Onoeman. Grabbing the gyrating sushi with chopsticks is not easy. We only scored one slice of raw tuna.

But the most educational items in the whole toy fair are the "new born babies" displayed by Dolly Dolls and Toys Factory of San Po Kong.

They are anatomically correct in every detail. Help your male yuplet develop inadequacy syndrome well ahead of his peers.

Child's play: There are a disturbing number of violent weapons at the toy fair this year, it seems to us. You can choose from replicas of the M-60 machine gun, an AK-47, a Schmeisser or an Uzi sub-machine gun at the Heep Tung Manufactory stand.

We noticed that most were made in brightly coloured plastic.

"You only make them in bright colours, so that they cannot be mistaken for the real thing?" we asked a representative of Heep Tung of Fo Tan.

"No, we have black ones as well," he replied, pulling out a realistic black M-16 automatic rifle.

Around the corner, Manley and Co of Cheung Sha Wan Road was showing an impressive array of toy handcuffs and guns, each piece emblazoned with the words: Official Police Play Equipment.

We find it hard to believe that the Royal Hong Kong Police feel the need to have official play equipment.

Surely they can just borrow their children's?

What a gas: The yukkiest toys of the year so far are being quietly assembled behind the factory doors of Mattel. Scheduled to be launched shortly are dolls which, er, expel internal gases – noisily – when their mid-sections are squeezed.

The dolls are based on popular US cartoon characters called Ren and Stimpy, and are expected to be BIG sellers, retailing at about US$15 each.

What did someone say about an ill wind not blowing anyone any good?

Gut feeling: Joe Lung, boss of Dataquest Hong Kong, took his family to Copenhagen recently, where he stumbled upon a restaurant named "Fart Plan".

Presumably this is where Ren and Stimpy eat.

Not amused: We would like to apologise in advance for all the digestive stories that are appearing on this page. There just seem to be a rash of them at the moment.

Skelgaard Jensen, a shipping man from Denmark who has been in Hong Kong for 20 years, wanted to de-mystify our story about a restaurant in his country called Fartplan. "Fart" in Danish is a completely innocent word meaning "move".

Most lift systems in Denmark are fitted with a sign which when lit says: "I Fart." It simply means "lift coming".

"The 'I Fart' signs were taped over when Queen Elizabeth II visited Copenhagen, in case they offended her," he said.

Officials were worried that she might think it was some sort of instruction.

Most undignified.

'S not nice: Oh dear. We hear that Kenner products is going to change the names of some of its new "Savage Mondo Blitzer" toy line, because they are allegedly offensive.

Adults in the US have complained. The plastic wheeled figures are called Eye Pus, Loaded Diapers, Snot Shot and Projectile Vomit.

A Kenner spokesman said the firm had received no complaints from consumers (children) during test sales. But after complaints from adults, cowardly executives have agreed to change some of the names.

What a shame. There's nothing children like better than items adults have decreed too naughty for them.

It's a rap: At the '93 Toy Fair we were pleased to find that not all dolls emit gas when you press their tummies.

A troll from Deep Source Ltd of Hong Kong forecasts the future. You make a wish and press its tummy. Light-bulbs in its eyes flash green and red. The instructions say that if the green light remains on "your wish may come true".

Not exactly sticking its neck out, is it? If his eyes stay red, your wish may come true anyway. The red eyes reminded us too much of the *Business Post* editor, so we moved on.

Warning to parents of children who like pop music: the toy industry has come up with probably the most infuriating device ever designed.

Many firms were showing The Rap Box, all furiously copied from each other.

This looks like a personal stereo, except it has a large red or green light on one side. Turn it on, and the light starts to flash and you hear a beat go chrr-chucka-chrr-chucka-chrr-chucka-chrr-chucka etc.

Touch other buttons on the machine, and more sounds join the rhythm: chrr-chucka-chrr-THUNK-THUNK-THUNK-chrr-chucka-chrr-chucka-BOOM.

"I've had this on for half an hour already," a youthful stall-holder clutching a pulsating Rap Box told an adult passer-by. She gave him a withering look of pity and moved on.

Some things only young people understand.

TWISTED HUMOUR

When we ran a competition in Hong Kong inspired, okay copied, from a US magazine, to change the meaning of a film by altering one letter, many people told us it was too hard.

Then the sackloads of mail started arriving. Here are a few:

From Pete Gallo of Sai Wan Ho:

The Frying Game: A look at vendors of chicken feet and bean curd in Hong Kong.

Done With the Wind: An epic tale about the unfortunate San Fernando Yacht Race.

Live and Let Dip: A Hong Kong Tourist Association film promoting scuba diving in Hong Kong harbour as an excellent excuse to stay an extra day.

Dive and Let Die: A Government information film advising against scuba diving in Hong Kong harbour, made with the support of the Hospital Authority.

Bag Trouble in Little China: Trade mark infringement drama about a factory in Taiwan and handbags that Louis Vuitton was none too pleased about.

You Only Love Twice: A Government film about the AIDS risk.

From Bob Palitz of Metro Broadcast:

Coldfinger: Horror film featuring a sadistic proctologist. (Ouch.)

Tonal Recall: Gweilo has brain transplant so he can pronounce Cantonese properly.

Done With the Wind: End of the typhoon season.

Empire of the Sum: The story of Peat Marwick.

The Codfather: The dark side of Harry Ramsden's rise to success.

Three Days of the Condom: A long weekend in Bangkok.

Germs of Endearment: Social diseases in the 1990s.

Apocalypse Cow: Expose of the meat industry by vegetarian crusaders. "Vegelantes, if you will," added Bob.

From Nigel Reid of Ernst and Young:

Oh! What a Lovely Bar: Full-length feature shot in Club Bboss.

Patman: More adventures from Hong Kong's hero.

The Ping and I: Memoirs from the diary of a Joint Liaison Group member.

The Man Who Would be Ping: The Martin Lee biography.

The Rattle of Britain: An in-depth review of JLG negotiating techniques.

Night Cheat: More goings-on in Wan Chai girlie bars.

Lien: A guide to Hong Kong landlord and tenant legislation.

From John Fuery of Dentsu, Young and Rubicam:

The Dours: A movie about the Liberal Party.

The Whining: A remake of the above.

Drear Window: A film about a pro-Beijing English language weekly.

From Mike Wray of Caldecott Road:

A Fist Full of Collars: Life in a Hong Kong laundry.

To Be the Pest: The Chris Patten story, as made by China.

Occidental Hero: The Chris Patten story, as made by Britain.

From Diccon Martin of Towry Law International:

Hamburger Bill: An Arkansas hillbilly bites off more than he can chew.

Last Mango in Paris: French farmers ban all imported fruit.

High Lender: Banks and property dealers struggle to issue big mortgages.

From Dr Robert Dunlop of Pokfulam Medical Centre:

Back to the Suture: A retired surgeon is called to help in an emergency case.

The Elephant Fan: An ivory dealer reminisces about the good old days.

Gone With the Wand: A Hong Kong Philharmonic conductor packs his baton and flies off.

From Norman Wingrove, information technology specialist:

The Remains of the Bay: Story of Hong Kong's latest landfill project.

Diving Miss Daisy: Octogenarian southern belle wins gold medal at Olympics.

The Cold Devils: A novel about a group of eccentrics who live in Wales.

From David Peng of Happy Valley:

The Vast Emperor: Fat king loses throne.

From Alan Shirley of Tai Tam:

Abridger Too Far: Story of a Hong Kong censor.

F.T.: Tale of a pink, wrinkled alien.
On Golden Pong: Life afloat on Aberdeen harbour.
From Ray Branch of First Pacific Co:
Sleeping with the Enema: Tale of Hong Kong actresses A, B, C and D, who slept with a seriously constipated movie agent.

Last Temptation of Chris: Story set in 1997, of Li Peng's offer to Chris Patten to become the first Chief Executive of the Special Administrative Region.

Top Hun: Biography of the brilliant Mongolian warrior Attila.

From Tom Mawer of Taikoo Shing:

Hobocop: The story of a police chief who is reduced to begging after a government committee strips him of all perks, including his car number plate.

The Thirty-Nine Stops: Mass Transit Railway training video.

The Story of Ho: Zany casino magnate stars in gambling comedy.

Tie Herd: Stock exchange tower overrun by phone-toting terrorists in suits.

Silence of the Lams: Inside story of an ICAC case in which two brothers refuse to testify.

From Trevor Hollingsbee, a maritime security operative:

A Fridge Too Far: Manila-bound domestic servants haggle with airline staff over how many appliances they can carry on to the flight in their cabin baggage.

Where the Buoys Are: Incoming ships try to negotiate the daily changes in the harbour reclamation.

NAMING OF PARTS

I think you should know you are perusing the words of a Famous Person. I am not talking about international superstardom. No, I am talking about relative fame – the 15 minutes of so each of us is theoretically entitled to these days. My claim to fame? I've got my name in print. There it is, nestled at the front of this book.

The fact that you have decided that this book is a load of rubbish and you are going to throw it away almost immediately is neither here nor there.

These days, getting credit for something is important – and can be measured in hard currency. Part of the multi-million dollar packages for film people these days is the position of their name in the credits on screen.

This is why, when you go to a film these days, it starts like this.

Mark Duckburger
and

Harold Brainscan
(fade)
Present
(fade)
A Thomas Cashpockets
Production
(fade)
of a
Mike Wallet/Irving Eagleburger
film
(fade)
From
Tony Bonehead
Studios
(fade)
Elmer Crabtree's
(fade)
WEATHER BULLETIN
(fade)

That's seven people listed who claim overall credit for the production. And that's before you list any of the people who actually did any WORK on it.

Talking about film workers, I note with disgust the modern habit of crediting every two-bit technician who came near the studio. I mean, who cares who the "Best Boy" on the set was, and whose opinion was it, anyway? The Best Girl, presumably? And what is a Key Grip? And whose keys does he or she keep a tight hold on? And what about the ubiquitous Boom-Gaffer? Does the cinema-going public care who gaffs the booms? Someone in Hollywood seems to believe that people sit in cinemas saying: "Oh, NICE bit of boom-gaffing. Unmistakably the work of Todd Swizzlechops. Go for it, Todd."

Television has also caught the byline disease in a bad

way. Have you noticed how on *L.A. Law,* the opening credits appear later and later into the story? I know an *L.A. Law* addict who swears she saw an episode where somebody's name appeared after the ad break.

On TV, the later your name appears, the better. You know someone has really made it when you are watching the climactic scene and this is what happens. Hunky, dimple-chinned lawyer leans over to kiss pretty blonde district attorney. Their lips approach. Then, four words are superimposed on the screen:

BOOM-GAFFER: FLIP BURBLESON.

Record albums are another medium overloaded with credits — vast numbers of names which include someone who delivered a tuna sandwich to a technician during an out-take.

A pop group called Wax released an album on which all the lyrics were printed. But the title of the last track, *Credit Where Credit's Due,* had no lyrics: it was followed merely by the usual list of credits and thank-yous. When you actually play the album, you discover the last track is a rap number in which a rap artist adlibs from the list of credits.

The byline disease has long had a firm hold on the publications industry, but it is now reaching extremes. In American magazines, such as *New York* and *Esquire,* the writers of the main features now have their names printed on the covers as part of the headlines. Instead of "Man Murdered" it now says: "Man Murdered By Investigative Reporter Brad Floop".

In newspapers all over the world, including Hong Kong's *South China Morning Post,* it has become house style in the introductory blurbs to have the reporter's name in capital letters, but the same is NOT true for the interviewee's name. So if a reporter got the ultimate scoop, the blurb would say:

Bestselling Author and

Divine Being, God, reveals all to SIMON NONENTITY.

And finally, this trend has invaded advertising. An increasing number of agencies now have their own names in small letters down the sides of ads. I cannot understand why advertising people resisted temptation for so long. It can't be modesty (look how many awards they present to themselves).

I think everyone is just waiting for someone else to take the lead.

Expect to see an ad something like the following before long:

YUMMAGOO TASTES GOOD.

(By BBDD Handicam, Ruby and Needless Co. Typeface by Andy Gudge. Layout by Sandy Loopy. Written by Slop Prunestone. Creative director: Arnaldo Botch. Executive creator: Tarquin Knees. Sandwiches by Toots and the gang from Happy Eats. Ms Loopy's hair by Andre.)

Thanks for contributing to my moment of fame by reading this.

You can throw this book away now.